The Attachment Theory Workbook

THE

Attachment Theory Workbook

Powerful Tools to Promote

Understanding, Increase Stability

& Build Lasting Relationships

BY ANNIE CHEN, LMFT

ALTHEA
PRESS

For general information on our other products and services or to obtain technical support, please contact our Customer Care Department within the United States at (866) 744-2665, or outside the United States at (510) 253-0500.

Althea Press publishes its books in a variety of electronic and print formats. Some content that appears in print may not be available in electronic books, and vice versa.

Interior and Cover Designer: Jamison Spittler
Editor: Camille Hayes
Production Editor: Erum Khan

ISBN: Print 978-1-64152-355-4 | 978-1-64152-356-1

R1

Printed in Canada

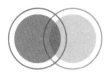

I dedicate this book to
my friend Annie Millar,
whose wisdom and joy
inspired many journeys
of awe-filled discovery.

Contents

Introduction ix

CHAPTER ONE   What's Your Attachment Style? 1

CHAPTER TWO   The Anxious Attachment Style 19

CHAPTER THREE   The Avoidant Attachment Style 49

CHAPTER FOUR   The Secure Attachment Style 85

CHAPTER FIVE   Attachment Style Interactions 113

CHAPTER SIX   Building a Secure Future 141

Blank Worksheets 149

Resources 178

References 179

Index 180

Introduction

What do you want from your closest relationships, and are you getting it? If you're like most of us, the answers to those questions might not be obvious. This workbook, based on an area of psychology called *attachment theory*, is designed to help you both answer those questions and work toward building more secure, lasting relationships with the people you care about most.

As a counselor who works with couples on relationship issues, I've seen the ideas in attachment theory brought to life, and I know firsthand the power the tools in this book have to heal people and bring them closer. But this book isn't just for couples; you can use the exercises and quizzes to better understand any significant relationship, whether it's with a parent, sibling, or close friend. All the exercises and strategies I present here are backed by evidence and experience; they have been proven effective for many people. My hope is that when you have finished working through this book— on your own, with a loved one, or both—you will better understand yourself and the people you care about. With the new skills you'll learn here and share with your loved ones, you can start down the path to healthier, more intimate, and more secure relationships. That, I believe, is what all of us want in the end.

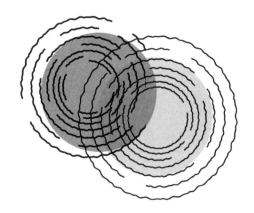

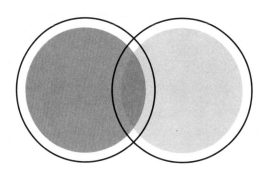

CHAPTER ONE

What's Your Attachment Style?

What Do You Want from Your Relationships?

As an adult, you have probably had dozens of important relationships over the years. I don't just mean romantic relationships—I also mean with parents, siblings, friends, and mentors. Of those significant emotional attachments, how many have been truly satisfying, secure, and lasting? Perhaps not as many as you'd like. But what if I told you there's a way to approach close relationships that would ensure secure, lasting intimacy? Would you experience the world, and approach intimacy, differently if you felt that security in your relationships was guaranteed? As it turns out, an individual's sense of security in relationships with others—what psychologists call *attachment style*—is a big determining factor in whether those relationships are successful or not. This workbook, based on the core insights from the field of attachment theory, is designed to help you discover your own attachment style and those of your loved ones, with the aim of learning healthier ways of relating to the most important people in your life.

Over the past 10 years, I've worked with hundreds of couples in my private practice, and issues of attachment style nearly always show up in one form or another. The challenges faced by these couples bring to life what I learned in graduate school. The tools and teachings presented in this book are a culmination of all that experience, and the exercises are designed to guide you to your own personal understanding of the experiences you have in your relationships and help you achieve the kind of security found in the most satisfying relationships.

If you're like most of us, you look back at some of your important relationships with fond memories, but there are also regrets: either things you didn't do well or times when others didn't come through for you. You can't change the past, but the good news is, you can change the *patterns* from your past that haven't served you well. Having perfect parents or a flawless relationship track record is not a prerequisite for building lasting, secure bonds. The only requirement for starting down the path to security and intimacy is your willingness to look honestly at your own behavior and believe that you can change. We have lots of evidence that putting effort into developing your relationships pays off. Studies show that having close, meaningful relationships is linked to better health, greater resilience, and more overall happiness in life. Consider the work you'll do with this book as an investment in a healthier, more secure future.

A note about relationship violence: This workbook can benefit anyone looking to gain insight about relationships, but if any of your relationships involves violence, I don't recommend this book alone as a solution. Although some violent behavior can result from attachment issues, there is generally much more going on that will require specialized help. Please address these issues with a counselor or advocate. If you are currently in a violent relationship, please seek the support you need. One way to start is by calling the National Domestic Violence Hotline: 1-800-799-7233.

Who Is Important to You?

Let's begin by identifying the relationships in your life that are important to you. These are the relationships you most want to benefit from the work you do here—the ones you'd most like to strengthen.

In the table below . . .
1. Write the names of the five most important people in your life.
2. Rate how important the relationship is to you, from 1 to 10 (where 10 = most important).
3. Rate how stressful the relationship is in your life, from 1 to 10 (where 10 = most stressful).
4. Finally, rank the list, beginning with 1 for the relationship you most want to work on improving.

Name of person	Who are they to you? What makes them a valued person in your life?	How important? (1–10)	How stressful? (1–10)	Priority to improve (1–5 rank)

Relationship Values

With those people in mind, consider what you really want from your relationships. At the end of your life, you'll be remembered for how you treated the people who are important to you. Imagine being surrounded by all the people you love and having them reflect on the positive qualities you fostered in your relationships with them. What would you want them to say? Write these positive relationship values below—for example, "honesty," "humor," "supportiveness"—and then rate yourself on how much you express these qualities *today* from 1 to 5, where 1 = needs great improvement and 5 = very satisfied.

The top five positive qualities and values I want to cultivate in my most important relationships:

1. _____   1   2   3   4   5

2. _____   1   2   3   4   5

3. _____   1   2   3   4   5

4. _____   1   2   3   4   5

5. _____   1   2   3   4   5

Before we dive into your relationships, let's consider what we mean by the different types of connection—or attachment—people can have in their close relationships. Perhaps you've heard about attachment style, and maybe you've even seen a self-help questionnaire that helps you sort yourself into a category. These attachment styles are based on psychological research. Let's do a quick overview now.

What Is Attachment Theory?

Researchers John Bowlby and Mary Ainsworth began developing the core of what became attachment theory in the mid-20th century. Their original theory says that infants develop better, socially and emotionally, when they form a close bond with a primary caregiver who's good at reading their cues and responding to their needs in a warm, sensitive, and timely way. At the time Bowlby and Ainsworth were developing their theory, the primary caregiver was usually the mother. Infants with this type of bond grow up trusting that others can help them feel safe, cared for, and supported in the world. This basic premise has been supported by over 60 years of attachment research and backed by experts in neuroscience, psychiatry, traumatology, and pediatrics.

Attachment researchers found that they could categorize the quality of relationships babies had with their main caregivers by observing how these babies responded to everyday stressful situations. Researchers grouped these responses into three distinct categories: *secure, insecure anxious,* and *insecure avoidant.*

The early researchers noted that when stressed, babies with *secure* attachment showed their distress in an observable way, but their response was not excessive. These babies seemed relaxed about seeking help and more often had interactions with their caregivers that ended in their being calmer and ready to move on from the stressful event.

Babies with *insecure anxious* attachment tended to respond to the same stressful events with more extreme crying and distress. They sought their caregiver but also appeared to reject the caregiver's attempts to provide relief. For these anxious babies, researchers observed more labored interactions that did not result in a fully soothed baby.

Babies with *insecure avoidant* attachment were less likely to cry during stressful situations and appeared indifferent about getting help from their caregivers. To the untrained eye, these babies looked fine, but researchers later discovered that elevated stress hormones in their bodies told a different story: They were affected by stress, but they didn't show it.

It may not surprise you to learn that babies grow into adults who develop versions of these *secure, anxious,* and *avoidant* attachments that can be readily identified in their relationships. Of course, adult relationships involve a lot more complexity, but it almost always boils down to this: When we get close to someone and come to depend on them, in stressful moments we show our true attachment style.

A fully accurate assessment of your attachment style is more complicated than this, but if you think about your closest relationships, you can probably get a basic sense of it. Think about close relationships you've had with romantic partners or in long-term friendships. In the course of those relationships, you've likely encountered a variety of stressors. During stressful times, if you typically expect that you can count on your relationship partners for help and comfort, then you have a secure attachment style. But let's say you encounter stress and don't have this natural expectation of safety and support. Maybe you aren't sure your relationship partners will help you, and you don't feel as if you can count on them to be there for you the way you need. If you've developed an insecure style, either anxious or avoidant, you are more likely to fear either being abandoned or being overwhelmed by the other person. As a result, you are less likely to engage in a way that makes you feel better. People typically have a characteristic attachment style that holds true across their close relationships, so securely attached people usually feel that their relationship partners are there for them; and people with either of the insecure attachment styles can look at their relationship history and see a string of unsatisfying relationships and perhaps regrettable actions.

After reading the descriptions of the secure, anxious, and avoidant styles, you may think, "I want the secure style!" And there's good reason to feel that way. People with a secure style of relating tend to feel more emotional safety with the people they're close to, are readier to collaborate, and are more resilient around conflict. But even these folks, under certain circumstances, can lapse into less adaptive ways of relating.

Regardless of the tendencies and attachment style you've developed to this point, you're not locked into these behaviors—your past doesn't have to dictate your future. Starting now, you can build stronger relationships. This workbook will help you . . .

- Recognize what specific attachment-related patterns and behaviors you and your loved ones have, especially under stressful or otherwise demanding circumstances.
- Learn new tools and practices to stop conflict escalation and reestablish safety and connection.
- Break old, unhelpful behavior patterns and start acting in ways that will build the lasting connections you want.

These skills are worth learning, because you'll get to spend more time enjoying what you love about the people you care about and be able to nurture more intimate, lasting bonds with them. And in times of difficulty and stress, you'll have resources you can call on when you need them.

What Is Attachment Theory Used For?

As a relationship therapist, I pay close attention to my clients' attachment styles, because attachment theory gives me a powerful way not only to identify behaviors that challenge a specific relationship, but also to see the pattern of how and why these behaviors show up across relationships, in both the past and present.

Does this early-learned attachment style drive *all* relationships *all* the time? Of course not! However, the relationships that are most affected by our early experiences are often the most significant ones, that is, the longer-term relationships that we rely on for emotional support. People in our lives whose roles more closely resemble the ones our parents played when we were young—nurturer, supporter, personal fan club—are most affected by our attachment style. Romantic partnerships usually fall under this category and are therefore prime candidates for replaying those habitual patterns we learned early in life. But it's also possible for attachment patterns to show up with other people, like close friends, family members, bosses and other authority figures, and colleagues and collaborators.

Your attachment style is essentially a blueprint of your basic assumptions about safety and trust. Although it may sound simple, your attachment style can have far-reaching consequences. Safety and trust often determine whether you can successfully collaborate, give and receive support, and handle conflict, so attachment theory gives us a simple schematic for understanding the basic building blocks that each person contributes to the foundation of a relationship.

Finding Your Attachment Style

Before you take the quiz to discover your personal attachment style, I want to emphasize that it's a tool to help you explore yourself and your relationships. It will not produce an official diagnosis of any kind or tell you anything definitive about yourself or other people, because real people are more complex than can be captured by a single assessment. With that in mind, this quiz is based on my study of attachment theory, on psychological research, and on my years of clinical experience observing people in their most revealing relationships.

This two-part quiz will help you understand where you fall on the attachment spectrum. Each part assesses a different aspect of attachment, and both are important to get the kind of nuanced picture that will be most useful to you. Please complete both parts of the assessment, which should take 10 to 15 minutes.

Attachment Quiz

Begin by thinking of one particularly important person in your life and the relationship you have with them. This person can be in a relationship with you currently or in recent memory. Unless otherwise stated, the terms *partner* and *relationship* will reference this relationship.

This quiz has been adapted to an interactive online format for your convenience. To take it anonymously and receive automatic scoring and results visit: www.attachmentquiz.com/quiz. If you take the quiz online, after reading your results, skip ahead to "Getting the Most Out of This Book" on page 16.

PART 1: Attachment Insecurity/Security

This part of the quiz explores how you feel and think about relationships. You will first address items that focus on your feelings (your insecurity score) and then items that focus on the things you think and do to make your relationship secure (your security score).

RATING SCALE *Using the scale below, rate each of the following statements:*

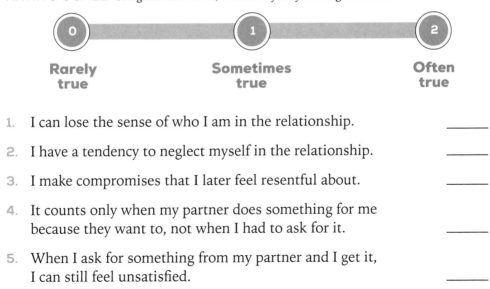

0	1	2
Rarely true	Sometimes true	Often true

1. I can lose the sense of who I am in the relationship. _____

2. I have a tendency to neglect myself in the relationship. _____

3. I make compromises that I later feel resentful about. _____

4. It counts only when my partner does something for me because they want to, not when I had to ask for it. _____

5. When I ask for something from my partner and I get it, I can still feel unsatisfied. _____

6. I feel misunderstood by my partner. _____

7. When my partner falls through on a promise, I can take it very personally. _____

8. I find it upsetting when my partner perceives something I do as unloving even though I mean really well. _____

9. I worry about whether my partner and I are fundamentally too different. _____

10. I struggle for a long time before I will ask for help. _____

11. When I imagine my parents, it's difficult to picture either of them looking back at me in an adoring and proud way. _____

12. It really gets under my skin when something feels unfair in the relationship. _____

TOTAL Add up the numbers for your total **insecurity** score: _____

Understanding Your Insecurity Score

These statements explored the way you respond *emotionally* to difference, complexity, and attachment stress in relationships. The higher your insecurity score, the more likely it is that close relationships can feel overwhelming for you.

14–24: High. You struggle with intimate relationships to the point of instability. When something stressful happens, you are quick to assume that your partner is against you, and you typically react to that assumption in self-fulfilling ways.

7–13: Moderate. Close relationships can be stressful for you. The more you depend on someone, the more confusing and stressful things can get. A fear of abandonment or feeling trapped can feel real at times, even when your partner gives you reasonable assurances.

0–6: Low. You're comfortable being alone, but you do your best when you have the love and support of a relationship.

Now we turn from issues of *emotional* insecurity to the ways you *actively work* to achieve security in your relationships. These items are more about your beliefs and behaviors than the way you feel.

RATING SCALE *Using the scale below, rate each of the following statements:*

1. It's easy to balance separateness and togetherness in the relationship. _____

2. My partner can change and grow as needed, and it's not a threat. _____

3. It's easy for me to make commitments to my partner and honor those commitments. _____

4. I need my partner as much as they need me. _____

5. If something is not working out with my partner, I can be patient and wait for the right solution to present itself. _____

6. We can have conflict even though neither of us is at fault. _____

7. I tell my partner everything. If there's something I haven't mentioned, it's because I'm absolutely certain it wouldn't bother them. _____

8. When my partner and I disagree, I commit to finding a win-win solution. _____

9. When I put my needs on hold so I can fully hear my partner, I'm confident those needs will eventually be addressed. _____

10. I can just ask my partner for what I want, and it usually works out one way or another. _____

11. When my partner and I fight, I take the lead to help us both feel okay again. _____

12. When past relationships have ended, it was a mutual and well-considered decision. _____

TOTAL Add up the numbers for your total **security** score: _____

Understanding Your Security Score

An important thing to understand about this score is that these things can be learned, if they aren't already natural to you. Even if you scored high on the *insecurity* scale, you *can* have secure-functioning relationships.

18–24: High. Your relationships are a resource for you, and that's partly because you do your best to ensure that you and your partner are taking care of each other. You usually take the high road when people aren't acting their best. No matter how stressful things get, you just try not to go there. A high security score paired with a low insecurity score indicates a secure style of attachment, which will be covered in chapter 4.

9–17: Moderate. Relationships are important to you, and you try your best to show up as your best self. You may even know exactly how to handle a difficult relationship, but when things get stressful, all that goes out the window. You know you can do better and that the relationships in your life are worth the effort.

0–8: Low. You've had difficulty building relationships that are stable and secure. The good news is that with information and practice, you can improve your ability to cultivate healthy, more satisfying relationships.

PART 2: Expressing Insecurity

This part of the quiz will help you explore how often you express insecurity in anxious or avoidant patterns. Even if your scores so far have suggested a secure attachment style, we all respond to stress in a variety of ways, so this part of the quiz is for everyone. Each item presents two options; please check the option that is more often true for you. When relevant, continue to think of the same relationship you chose in part 1.

It's harder for me to be patient when . . .

☐ People aren't understanding me.

☐ I feel stuck doing something I don't enjoy.

When beginning a new relationship that could be significant, it's a deal breaker if the person . . .

☐ Doesn't make an effort.

☐ Comes on too strong.

Conflict is . . .

☐ An opportunity to get something off my chest.

☐ Usually unproductive.

When I get upset at my partner, I . . .

☐ Have to express myself to them.

☐ Prefer to figure it out on my own.

In the relationship, I'm at my worst when I feel . . .

☐ Abandoned or rejected.

☐ Pressured or intruded upon.

In the relationship, I want to feel . . .

☐ As connected to my partner as possible.

☐ At ease.

When I'm overwhelmed, I feel better when I . . .

☐ Vent to someone.

☐ Find distraction in something else (exercise, substances, work, etc.).

There are certain things I don't tell my partner, because . . .

☐ They could get upset
and reject me.

☐ It's my business—they
don't need to know.

My partner is more likely to complain that I . . .

☐ Criticize and find fault
with them.

☐ Am not as engaged as
they want me to be.

When we spend time apart, I . . .

☐ Feel sad or lonely.

☐ Feel relieved to have
time to myself.

When I feel hurt by my partner, I recover . . .

☐ When I get what I need
from them.

☐ Pretty quickly on my own.

It would upset me more if my partner told their friends . . .

☐ Nothing about me.

☐ Something embarrassing
about me.

To Score
Count the number of check
marks directly above, then
multiply by 2 for your score.

_____ = **anxious** style score

To Score
Count the number of check
marks directly above, then
multiply by 2 for your score.

_____ = **avoidant** style score

If one of your scores is 18 or higher, this is likely to be your dominant style of expressing relationship insecurity. If both your scores were lower than 18 then neither may be dominant; you express some combination of both styles. You'll learn more about what this means in the chapters dedicated to the anxious style (chapter 2) and the avoidant style (chapter 3). Both chapters will be useful, even if your score on one style is higher.

Getting the Most Out of This Book

In addition to helping you understand your own personal attachment patterns and tendencies, this book will also help you recognize the patterns of the people closest to you. If you scored high on either *anxious style* or *avoidant style* in part 2 of the Attachment Quiz, you might prefer to skip to the relevant chapter to explore what that means and what you can do about it.

To get the most from this book and maximize what it can do for you, plan on working through all the chapters eventually. You're likely to have relationships with people running the entire spectrum of attachment styles, from secure to insecure, anxious to avoidant, so the other chapters will help you understand those styles. In addition, attachment styles exist on a continuum, so while your scores might overall indicate secure attachment, for example, perhaps your score on *insecure anxious* was also somewhat high. Finally, different people—for example, two romantic partners—can bring out different tendencies in you, in part as a response to their own attachment styles. Careful study of all the chapters will give you the most benefit.

The exercises in this workbook are meant to encourage awareness and understanding of yourself and others. As you complete the exercises, if your personal history with relationships brings up memories that are troubling or sensations that are overwhelming, please stop reading or writing and do something that helps you feel grounded, whether that's doing the dishes, taking a walk, calling a friend, or doing a quick mindfulness meditation. You can return later to the exercise, after you feel calmer or enlist the support of a counselor to further explore the themes in this book and your responses to them.

Finally, I recommend building in breaks for yourself. Don't try to complete the entire workbook in one sitting! Make sure you get enough sleep, eat well, drink water, see friends, and go out and take breaks to do something active. Not only will breaks make the process more enjoyable, but you'll also have time for the material to sink in as you work your way through the book.

Chapter Recap

- Attachment theory simply explains the stress that people do or don't experience when they are dependent on others in relationships. It is not a horoscope or explanation of personality.

- The patterns that people have in response to this stress are a natural progression of what they have experienced in relationships since they were very young.

- The patterns of behavior for people with insecure attachment can cause trouble in relationships.

- This book can help you examine your responses and explore the possibilities for real change.

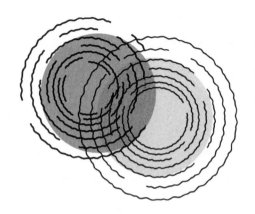

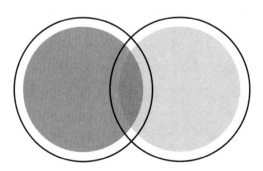

CHAPTER TWO

The Anxious Attachment Style

If your score on part 2 of the Attachment Quiz (page 14) placed you in the anxious style, this chapter will help you learn more about what that means and what you can do about it. The higher you scored, the more likely you are to express any relationship insecurity you feel with anxiety. After a description of the traits associated with this attachment style, the information and exercises in this chapter will help you see how this style plays out in your relationships (whether you are anxiously attached or your partner is), learn to accept yourself and others, develop the skills to communicate clearly, and learn how to strengthen your relationship in ways that will leave you feeling more secure.

Traits of the Anxious Style

Attachment theory is concerned with safety and trust in intimate relationships. Considering your score on the *insecurity* part of the quiz, the higher your score, the harder it can be to feel consistently safe and trusting in your close relationships, and the more likely it is that they could be negatively impacted by your anxious attachment patterns. If your *insecurity* score was low, then even if you had the maximum score for the anxious style, your anxious patterns may only infrequently have a negative effect on your relationships.

People with an anxious attachment style . . .

- Can be incredibly generous and attentive to those they care about.
- Are sensitive to what they perceive as abandonment.
- Will readily tell someone how they feel.
- Tend to blame their feelings on others ("You made me feel this way!").

The biggest fear for people with an anxious style of attachment is abandonment. When this fear is triggered, even in small ways, they can panic. They may express their need for support, but the way they communicate this might end up pushing away the very person they want support from. They can be quick to feel hopeless and show their disappointment preemptively. Because of this, even when their need is urgent, their way of seeking support can come off as alarming or off-putting to others.

Here are some examples of people I've worked with in my practice who have an anxious attachment style. Please note that in the examples throughout this book, all identifying details have been changed.

Asha was in her early 20s and noticed a pattern in her life: She would make a good friend and become very close to them, but within a couple of years, they would grow apart due to her anger and jealousy about that friend taking on interests and friendships that didn't include her.

Nora's husband, Damian, was a firefighter who worked 48-hour shifts. They had a great time when he was home, but when he left for work, Nora struggled and felt depressed. She texted him often for updates about what he was doing. If Damian didn't respond within a few minutes, Nora's anxiety worsened.

Bruno was an outgoing person who'd started to date again after his last relationship ended with a lot of turmoil. In the past, he'd jumped "all in" from the first sign of a connection, but he'd become apprehensive about doing that again. He wanted to figure out how to be his passionate, expressive self without making the same mistakes as before.

Remember, attachment styles exist on a spectrum, and many people with insecure attachment display both anxious and avoidant patterns at various times. You might also recognize important people in your life—parents, former or current romantic partners, or others—in these pages.

Self-Awareness

The following sections and exercises are designed to help you identify your anxious patterns. I invite you to read this chapter with an attitude of curiosity about yourself and your important relationships, rather than blame or criticism. Being open and curious is the best way to learn new information about yourself and fuel your motivation to change behaviors that don't serve you.

HOW ANXIOUS ATTACHMENT FEELS TO YOU

There are common experiences among people who form anxious attachments. As you read the description in this section, consider how closely it resembles your experiences in relationships. If an aspect doesn't match exactly, don't worry about it. However, in the places you *do* recognize yourself, you might feel comforted to know that you are not alone. The patterns I'm describing here are very common.

If you have an anxious style, you like the *idea* of attaching to people, and romantic attachment in particular is very attractive to you. Something just feels right about having someone special to confide in, support, and be supported by. Your fantasy of an ideal relationship is one where your partner just "gets" you, down to your core. When you start a new relationship, it's important to you that there is the promise or possibility of feeling truly understood. If you feel understood, then you can attach and be long-term friends or partners. You're unlikely to want to pursue the relationship if you don't feel attended to or if the other person doesn't "get" you.

Trouble can start once you settle into commitment. The person who seemed so promising at first, attentive and understanding, eventually skips a beat or gets distracted with other things, and that's when you remember that people aren't always what they seem. You've had a script running since childhood about what to expect when you depend on someone, and it sounds something like, "I need them . . . but they will disappoint me." You're driven by your desire to connect, which often means you overfocus on the other person, always putting them first, while feeling unhappy about your own needs not being met. You want to give and receive, with maximum connection.

When you begin to feel anxious in the relationship, you feel the hurt deeply, even for minor incidents—as though the betrayal you fear has already happened. In those moments, you truly need and want support. You can imagine getting that support, but your stomach churns with doubt that the person you love will be there for you. The connection you crave always seems just out of reach, even when you're trying hard to get it. This adds to your distress. You've probably said to yourself, more than once, "I just don't know what to do anymore."

When your anxious style is on full display, you threaten the relationship, make ultimatums, and say and do things you later regret, like "I hate you," "I want a divorce," or "You don't give a shit about me." You're not proud of this behavior, but when you're in the moment, you don't feel that you have a choice. You need to show how much pain you're in. You hope the person you love will notice and finally give you the feeling of security you crave; instead, your behavior pushes the person away.

Eventually the crisis passes, and you iron things out. But the incident has reinforced a familiar hurt and assumption: The people you love can't be depended on. You still want that connection, but you wonder if you're too needy for anyone to want to deal with you. You know you ask for extra, but you also *give* extra.

Attachment theory teaches us that you *learned* this model of giving and receiving, even when it might not have been appropriate. Perhaps when you were a child, you were put in an unfair position to help a parent feel better when they were having a hard time. Of course, you complied at the time, because that's what we do when our survival is dependent on the well-being of someone else—we pitch in. But developmentally, when you're asked to do this before you have the resources to take care of yourself, you're doing it out of a sense of survival anxiety, which can then be built into your blueprint of what's needed to get love from someone. Hence, it's familiar to you to play rescuer and overperform—as well as overdemand—in your closest relationships.

You might have memories from childhood of being unhappy with the amount of attention and care you received from one or both of your parents. You had at least one caregiver, even if it was a grandmother or nanny, who was there in significant ways during important and formative times, and you remember some of the ways you felt truly loved. But this was an inconsistent experience; you couldn't rely on love being there when you needed it. It's the same inconsistency that drives you bonkers now, when relationships deepen and your dependence on another person increases.

How Well Does That Description Fit You?

Remember that no single description can apply perfectly to anyone, but if your score suggests anxious attachment, you probably recognized yourself as you read the previous description. When you consider some of your most important experiences in close relationships, how accurate would you rate the description for yourself? Circle the number that corresponds to your rating.

Not at all accurate   **Completely accurate**

Which parts of that description were most true for you?

_____

_____

_____

_____

_____

_____

HOW ANXIOUS ATTACHMENT PLAYS OUT IN RELATIONSHIPS

People who are anxiously attached are known for acting out when their anxiety gets triggered. They don't do it on purpose; they're just responding to their own distress in their characteristic way. They may or may not even be aware of their patterns of reaction and can be quick to be critical and abrasive when they've been triggered. They act impulsively in relationship-threatening ways, which ultimately works against their efforts at maintaining a stable and loving bond.

People with anxious attachment can also contradict themselves. They want your support, but when they're triggered, they feel so upset they can barely be around you. Relationships with anxiously attached individuals tend to have more ups and downs. Their anxiety breeds cycles of giving, resentment, complaint, demanding, temporary satisfaction, and giving again.

When people try to get their needs met through blaming, anger, guilt, or nagging, they rarely realize in the moment how much this approach stresses out those around them and burns through their _relationship capital_, the goodwill people build together that allows the relationship to handle challenges. Marriage researcher John Gottman has determined that for every negative feeling or interaction couples have, it takes at least five positive ones to restore the balance for a happy, healthy relationship. To restore peace, people might give in because they are getting the benefit of giving—a positive approach that can strengthen a relationship—but they may give in because they feel under duress. Ultimately, this demanding approach to getting what they want burns through relationship capital.

This dynamic was a struggle for a couple I'll call Jorge and Tanya. Jorge and Tanya had been together eight years. Both had stressful jobs, Jorge in academia and Tanya as a corporate lawyer. Jorge typically got home first and had to wait for Tanya to get off work, which was usually a few hours later. When she got home, Jorge was eager to talk, but Tanya just wanted to unwind with dinner and a movie. Sensing Jorge's anxiety, she started engaging her own more avoidant tendencies by finding ways to put off these often-long evening debriefs with Jorge. She might stop at the grocery store on the way home or take the dog out for a walk as soon as she walked in the door. By the time she was "available" to him, he was frustrated and demanding.

"You're not even paying attention," he would complain. Tanya was very put off by this but tolerated it, because otherwise it would turn into a bigger fight.

From Jorge's perspective, he wasn't doing anything intentionally counterproductive or unkind; he was just trying to feel more connected to Tanya. Jorge was expressing himself in the manner that felt natural and familiar to him. But he hadn't realized the effect it had on Tanya or how stressful their relationship had become for her. The simmering conflict cost them a lot of relationship capital, and in the end, there were not enough positive interactions to rebuild it.

Unrestrained anxious behaviors and communication patterns put strain on a relationship and burn through relationship capital. If the capital isn't replenished, your relationship might not end, but you'll both eventually feel the effects of that stress on the quality of your bond.

Let's turn now to an exercise that will help you understand what your anxious attachment behavior is really about. You'll dig deep into an uncomfortable experience, but the goal is to help you understand how this attachment style works in your relationships.

1. Think of something that happened in a relationship that made you feel bad or uncomfortable. What happened to trigger this feeling? Examples:

   My boss got mad when I was late to a meeting because I was sick with food poisoning.

   My partner made fun of me in front of a friend.

   The incident that triggered my bad or uncomfortable feeling:

   _____

   _____

2. Incidents hurt people for reasons that are personal to each individual. If we zoom in on your experience of the event you just noted, what was the worst part about it *to you*?

   _____

   _____

   _____

Examples:

Someone I looked up to disapproved of me.

Someone got mad at me before I could explain myself.

I felt ashamed about something I couldn't help or change.

I felt like I couldn't do anything right.

The worst part about the incident for me:

_____

_____

Nice job for allowing yourself to be curious about your own feelings and experiences, and why they affect you uniquely! This understanding is an important part of being able to manage your feelings.

Here's a bonus exercise; while it's optional, it can be extremely helpful in understanding the pattern of this feeling across your life. Below is a timeline from birth to 20 years of age. The first couple of decades of our experiences can be very formative. If we didn't have help managing the difficult things we thought and felt during this time, they can affect how we view others and ourselves later in life.

Consider your first two decades of life. When was the first time you recall having the feeling or experience, or one similar to it? Put an *X* on that part of the timeline.

1	2	3	4	5	6	7	8	9	10	11	12	13	14	15	16	17	18	19	20

Age

Most incidents that evoke big feelings do so because those feelings have their origin in early life. Did you put an *X* somewhere on this timeline? If so, this is very normal. Now go forward on the timeline and put an *X* on the different ages when you remember having this same feeling. Try to put at least three *X* marks on the timeline and as many as you would like. Consider experiences you've had with people at home, school, work, church, and so on.

Put down your pen or pencil and take a deep breath. You are now viewing the legacy of this feeling or experience in your life. Take a look at the timeline and consider the following questions:

1. How does it look overall? Are there more *X* marks concentrated in one area, or are they spread out?
2. Did anything surprise you?
3. Are there certain kinds of relationships where you tend to experience this feeling more?
4. Has anyone or anything ever helped you go through this feeling with more ease?

Awareness of Others

Attachment patterns also emerge under stress for others in your relationships. Learning about yourself is only part of the equation; the other part is knowing and understanding what kind of attachment patterns are playing out for the person you're in a relationship with. This will give you the best chance at managing conflict and preventing misunderstandings. In chapter 5, we'll explore all combinations of attachment style pairings, but for now let's explore how you feel if your *relationship partner* is anxiously attached.

HOW IT FEELS WHEN OTHERS ARE ANXIOUSLY ATTACHED

Being in a relationship with someone who is acting out an anxious attachment style can feel like dealing with an angry customer while staffing a support desk. When people are in anxious patterns of attachment, their *expressiveness* increases; that is, they let you know, either verbally or through their actions, that they're unhappy. Their complaints may even be justified, but they can come across as angry or critical, which makes it hard to respond with kindness. After a while, if you are the only one on duty at that customer service desk, you can feel overwhelmed and demoralized. If you have a history of being treated unfairly, you might even feel abused by the other person's anxious demands.

Even if you are normally very capable, you might find it difficult to stand up for yourself in the middle of a conflict with someone who is anxiously attached. Insecure anxious people are generally good at talking and making their argument. In fact, many talk so much because silence makes them *more* anxious.

If you love the person, a part of you might really want to do something helpful and supportive. Another part of you might not want to, because they really don't seem that loveable or loving in the moment, right? Or perhaps the person's behavior triggers your own attachment-related stress patterns, because the person you depend on so much is mad at you.

Many people will react to this dynamic in one of two ways: Either they will try really hard to make their anxious loved one happy, or they will under-respond and check out in order to protect themselves from attack. Neither response is particularly sustainable in the long term. The first approach, without appropriate awareness and boundaries, will burn you out, and the second approach will just make the anxious individual even more anxious.

Over the longer term, it can feel as if the anxiously attached person is chronically negative and ultimately impossible to satisfy. They always have something to complain about, even if you do everything you can to meet their needs.

Here are some frequent complaints I hear about people exhibiting anxious attachment behavior:

- They are angry, abrasive, critical, and demanding.
- They are not satisfiable. There is always something wrong.
- They're "high maintenance."

These behaviors can be a turnoff. During low moments, your morale about the relationship can sink. If these low moments happen often enough, you start to wonder whether the relationship is worth all the effort. These things are common in intimate relationships with people with anxious attachment, but there are some things you can do to ensure you don't burn out.

Recognizing Relationship Burnout

The first step is recognizing what's happening when it's still early enough to fix it. What are the signs that you may be giving too much and getting burned out? Learning to recognize these signs is a good way to monitor your energy and boundaries without blaming or judging what someone else is doing.

For each behavior, make one check mark if you notice it happens in relationship *sometimes* and two check marks if it happens *often*:

_____ Criticize yourself or the other person

_____ Think obsessively about the other person

_____ Get distracted from things you're doing, like work

_____ Forget to exercise

_____ Neglect to eat well

_____ Lose sleep

_____ Lose interest in activities you like

_____ Feel you don't have enough time with other people in your life

_____ Feel resentful

_____ Feel depleted

_____ Feel depressed

_____ Feel anxious

_____ Feel you can't fully be yourself

_____ Feel fearful

_____ Feel you always have to be "on"

_____ Feel you can't say no

_____ Feel a certain sensation in your body (e.g., headache, tension, numbness): _____

_____ Other: _____

Your check marks might be good indicators that you've reached a limit with something. If you allow this to continue, it could affect you and eventually the relationship in negative ways. Try to address the issues where you can, by making sure you exercise, eat well, and seek medical care when needed. For those problems that are more complicated to address, like tension or resentment, learn to recognize them as the early signs that you should talk to your partner about how to start making changes.

HOW TO RESPOND TO ANXIOUS ATTACHMENT IN OTHERS

Remember, anxious attachment reactions are about fear of abandonment and doubts that a relationship need will be met. Anxious attachment behaviors can surprise you, because they seem overblown relative to the perceived threat. These reactions can even surprise the people they come from!

It's important to remember that people we love who react in unpleasant ways when they're unhappy or feel abandoned aren't doing it on purpose. They may not even know they're having a big impact on you. Most are not fully aware of how they're coming across. They're just expressing themselves in a way that's familiar to them and trying to get their needs met.

Take a look at how Tom helped his partner, Sanjay, manage an anxious attachment dynamic. Sanjay and Tom had recently moved in together after getting engaged five months earlier. Even though Sanjay was happy about the engagement, the idea of permanently depending on Tom triggered Sanjay's anxious attachment. He was often in a bad mood, and his irritation came out as criticism. Sanjay had a litany of complaints, including that Tom was a "slob." Sanjay delegated cleaning tasks to Tom and criticized Tom's effort when it wasn't up to his standard. Tom had not done much to improve the dynamic, either. He simply complied when told to do something, passively waited for the inevitable complaint, and then silently stewed while Sanjay criticized.

In therapy, they were able to try something different. After agreeing that Tom would mop the floors, they tried a new approach.

"How do the floors look this week?" Tom asked.

"Not good." Sanjay made a look of disapproval.

"What specifically isn't good enough?" Tom persisted.

"I can still see dirt in the corners," he replied. "You just don't pay enough attention. I knew this wouldn't work. Now I have to redo them anyway."

"Stop," Tom said clearly. "You don't have to do that. The floors are my job. Tell me what isn't working, and I'll get to it in the next few days."

Sanjay breathed a sigh of relief and felt better. The floors still weren't to his exact standard, but at least now he could count on his partner.

In this interaction, Tom learned that Sanjay's attachment anxiety was activated so he took the lead to guide them through it. Rather than staying passive, Tom actively sought feedback, gave Sanjay a directive ("Stop"), and set an expectation ("I'll get to it in the next few days"). This set a new pattern, which had a better outcome for both of them.

Soothing Anxious Attachment

Following Tom and Sanjay's lead, this exercise will help you identify your own way of approaching conflict with someone in your life who is anxiously attached. Think of someone in your life who can be rather abrasive and express their needs in a critical or pessimistic way. What is your natural response when they behave this way?

_____

_____

_____

How do they usually respond in return?

_____

_____

_____

With that pattern identified, think about what behaviors might be more helpful for you when responding to anxious attachment. Here are some suggestions to help your loved one in a moment of panic and anxiety. Put a check next to the ones that you already do or have tried.

- ☐ Reassurance. "I'm here." "I'm not going anywhere."

- ☐ Proximity and contact in a way that is appropriate for the relationship. If the person is your romantic partner, use loving touch and embrace. If not, step forward, make kind eye contact and smile, or if appropriate, hold their hand.

- ☐ Take the lead. Help manage the person's anxiety with clear and simple directives. People in a state of panic are more primed for understanding short phrases. "Stop." "Slow down." "Tell me something nice." "Give me a moment to think."

- ☐ Pace their expectations and anticipation. "Let's talk about that in a few minutes, when we're calm." "We'll talk about that after we finish this."

- ☐ Ask for specific feedback. "How did the way we talked work for you this time?"

Which of these would you like to try the next time you encounter anxious behavior? Write them below, making them specific to your relationship with the anxious individual:

_____

_____

_____

_____

_____

Learning Acceptance

I applaud your courage and curiosity to learn about attachment insecurity and to explore attachment anxiety in your relationships, which may be something new for you. You've learned that your reactivity gets triggered in part because of the uncertainty you feel about depending on someone, and that reactiveness puts unnecessary strain on relationships and prevents intimacy. The next step is adopting an attitude of *acceptance*.

ACCEPTING YOURSELF

The mind tends to accept things it likes or is familiar with and to dismiss things it doesn't like or finds unfamiliar. This is normal, but it can make it difficult to adjust to new experiences and uncomfortable truths about ourselves, even if it means we continue doing things that aren't good for us or our relationships.

To make room for new behaviors, we have to have enough energy and motivation to change. Otherwise, we're not likely to put in the necessary work to adapt to new information and realities. Acceptance helps us make room for learning by freeing up the energy we had been using to resist or avoid things so that we can use that energy in more productive ways.

Map Your Emotions

Emotions have both a mental and a physical component, and we can feel resistant to one or the other or both. Directing our attention to the specific bodily experiences that are connected to an emotion can help facilitate greater acceptance of that emotion. Since anger is such a powerful emotion, try this next exercise to see how it works for you.

Recall the last time you were angry with someone close to you. Can you feel just a little of what it was like? Where do you feel it in your body? (Example: It's in my upper chest.)

_____

_____

_____

Imagine what size/shape/temperature/color/quality the feeling has. (Example: It feels like a swirling, confused ball that is stuck in my stomach.)

_____

_____

_____

When did it appear? (Examples: An hour ago. When I knew I wasn't going to get what I wanted.)

_____

_____

_____

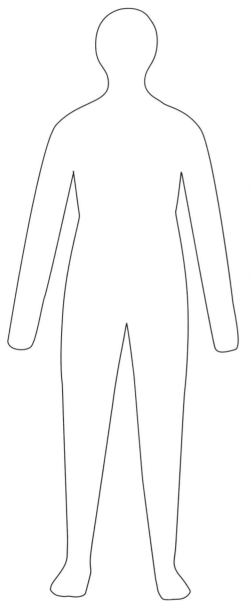

Using a pen or pencil, make a sketch of what you feel on the part of the body where you feel it.

Now, take a deep breath. Even imagining anger can bring the feeling into your body! Acknowledge that sometimes this feeling is in your body and sometimes it is not. Practice telling yourself that there's no need to fight it. When the feeling is there, try to accept its physical presence, and keep an open and even curious mind about what it is there for. Learning how to manage strong emotions in this way can be helpful when you are triggered.

Self-Compassion

As you wake up to the effects of your behavior in past relationships, you may also become more aware of the hurt that you caused, however big or small. While anxious behaviors may have been invisible to you before, or even necessary, you might now be more aware of how they affected the people you love and the relationships you put your heart and trust into. You may see more fully how you unintentionally hurt someone you care about during moments of distress. In order to change, we first have to find the courage to look at what isn't working rather than to blindly hate it or attack it mercilessly.

Self-compassion can be helpful when you feel this way. Practicing self-compassion means being sensitive to your own difficulties and suffering, and having a sincere desire to help that suffering.

Want to try a little self-compassion? Imagine a time you did or said something you regret. When you close your eyes, see yourself at the age when this incident happened. Watch the scene as if it were a movie, and imagine the camera zooming in to a close-up of you. Now, watch your face and body before, during, and after the incident. Watch the cascade of emotions as the entire scene plays out. Notice the expression of hurt, anger, frustration, fear, hopelessness, or contempt. Keep watching until the "you" in the scene reaches a still point, with the frame frozen on you. Now put a hand over your heart, and looking right into the eyes of the "you" in the scene, repeat one or more of the following phrases:

- "I see how you suffer just as anyone else does."
- "May you be happy."
- "May you be free from pain."
- Anything else that the "you" in the scene needs to hear in order to know that this difficulty is seen and acknowledged.

Now imagine the scene unfreezes, and all your kind and caring words have gone into the "you" in the scene. What effect do your words have? How do they make you feel?

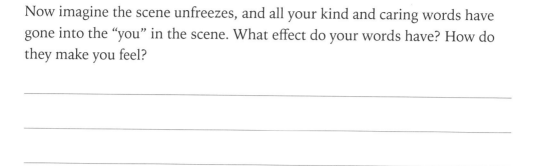

If self-compassion is unfamiliar to you, it might be because you've learned to condemn, judge, and criticize yourself in situations where you learn something you don't like about yourself. This is a common way to respond, but when it comes to healing attachment anxiety, self-condemnation is likely to produce only more insecurity and anxiety, not less. Continue to practice being compassionate toward yourself. Check out the Resources (page 178) for ways to develop this healing practice.

ACCEPTING OTHERS

Accepting yourself is only part of the process of working with this attachment style. Accepting another's attachment style means opening up to the reality of how they experience the world and how they have learned to react to it. It simply means paying attention and not judging what you learn. When you allow yourself to open up to this reality, you can deepen your relationships based on a fuller understanding of your loved ones.

Of course, accepting another's experience with anxious attachment does not mean you have to accommodate all the ways in which their reactive behavior affects the relationship. Sometimes acceptance simply means being willing to remind yourself that their anxious attachment patterns aren't about you. The following example shows this process in action.

Dominique is in her late 20s; her mother, Vero, raised Dominique mostly as a single mom. After Vero's husband passed away last year, Dominique noticed that her mother was calling her more often and depending on her for practical and emotional support. At first she didn't mind, and as a second-generation immigrant daughter, she felt it was her duty to take care of her mother. But after several months, Dominique grew increasingly frustrated with her mom's unspoken expectations and demands. Even visiting weekly wasn't enough; her mom wanted her to move in part-time.

Dominique didn't know how to say no, because she felt bad that her mom felt so alone. On top of everything else, when they spent time together, her mom was constantly critical of her life and career choices, which was understandably off-putting to Dominique. Pretty soon, Dominique found their relationship intolerable and didn't know how to get away.

Dominique had a breakthrough when she was able to remind herself in real time that her mom's clingy behavior wasn't about her. This reminder allowed Dominique to understand more clearly that her mother's behavior was due to her attachment style, and that understanding helped her accept what was happening in the relationship and even accept her mom more easily. Once she freed herself from the responsibility of her mom's experience, she reported that she felt less defensive and was actually able to talk to her mom in ways that were more soothing and helpful while maintaining her own boundaries. As a result of this acceptance, Dominique felt less stressed and trapped, and her mom got the help and compassion she needed.

Empathizing with Insecurity

So far, you've been taking in a lot of information about anxious attachment. This exercise will give you an opportunity to practice empathy so that you can *feel* it rather than just think about it.

One of the core conditions that most people say triggers their anxiety is inconsistency in the type of attention or care they can expect from their partners. Let's explore how this affects one's state of mind.

Imagine something in your life that you very much depend on every day. Perhaps it's a paycheck, a home, or even something as simple as the sunrise. Write a couple of sentences about this thing and why you are grateful for it.

Something I depend on every day that I am grateful for is . . .

_____

_____

_____

When I think of how it supports my well-being, I feel . . .

_____

_____

_____

Now, imagine that something has just changed. Through forces that you cannot control, the thing you just wrote about no longer works the way it should. Now, each time you expect it to be there, you could be met with shock and disappointment. If you wrote about a paycheck, then imagine that your salary mysteriously drops every time, by an unpredictable amount. If you chose your home, imagine that every time you get there, you're not sure if the key will unlock the door. Sometimes the lock just mysteriously changes. If you thought of the comfort of the sun coming up every day, imagine that daylight saving time is enforced in an unpredictable and variable way.

With every disappointment, you remember your anticipation of the warm comfort of how it was before, when things were normal. As you imagine this new reality, what do you feel?

_____

_____

Now imagine that you're going to lunch with someone you care about, and you're in the midst of this feeling. How would that lunch encounter be different than usual?

_____

_____

You can imagine this is how your loved one with anxious attachment might feel. The difference is, of course, that their perception of your reliability is the thing that leaves them feeling insecure, while at the same time, you are the person they choose to be close to.

Healthy Communication

As you read earlier, accepting the truth of how you or your relationship partner experiences attachment does not mean you have to accept the behaviors or impact of those behaviors in your relationships. Thinking specifically about your own attachment-related behaviors, you can *acknowledge* the anxious tendencies you have toward closeness and dependency, and *learn* skills that will help you find comfort and be soothing while also achieving your relationship goals.

One of these skills is healthy and clear communication. We've previously discussed how people with anxious attachment tend to project their upset when they are triggered, frustrated, or hurt. This communication often comes out in a blaming, demanding, or angry way, but with a hope that others will pick up on the underlying needs and meet them. This unfortunately is not a very reliable model for getting your needs met.

Sometimes it works, and that might reinforce your tendency to freewheel how you express your emotions. But consider this: If the way you communicate causes stress to your partner and therefore the relationship, it works because your partner loves you, not because you are being an effective collaborator in getting what you want. In fact, when you freewheel your emotions in a way that puts stress on your partner and the relationship, you are using up hard-earned relationship capital.

Communicating your feelings and needs in a more intentional and mutually beneficial way simply takes practice. It may not feel as gratifying in the short term as just blurting out something that will give you an immediate discharge of relief, but in the long term, it could help you maintain and strengthen a valued relationship. A bonus is that these tools will work in all your relationships.

Getting Consent to Express Yourself

When you are close to someone, what you do and say around that person makes an impact, whether positive or negative. There are no throwaways. To encourage effective collaboration and get your needs met in the relationship, you need to monitor interactions in real time and ensure the conversation stays productive. That said, it is also important to express yourself.

How do you do both? Getting consent is an important tool in a relationship when it comes to negotiating a balance between one person's needs and desires and another's limits of comfort. Practicing healthy consent ensures that you're talking about both sides of the dialogue. We learn about consent most often when it comes to physical and sexual boundaries in relationships. Before engaging in a sexual encounter, we check that the other person is ready and wants it, as well. But when it comes to intense interactions that involve the mind or emotions, we don't often consider getting consent. For the sake of relationships, we should.

Can you think of a conversation you've had in the past when you were in an anxious pattern that quickly escalated and nothing got done? Go back to that scene in your head.

Could adding one or more of the following communication tools have improved the feeling or outcome of the conversation, even by a little? Read the following list of suggestions and check as many as you imagine could have helped you get closer to what you wanted, while also respecting the other person's boundaries.

Suggestions for getting consent:

☐ State an intention and check if it's okay for the other person. "I want to make a complaint. May I have permission to do that with you?" "I have very strong feelings I need to express. Are you in a space to hear me?" "I have some thoughts about your situation. Would you like advice or for me to get involved?"

☐ Request what you want on a timeline that is comfortable for the other person. "Can you let me know when you are ready to discuss the remodel project?"

☐ Request a specific amount of time for the conversation and stick to it. "Can you take 20 minutes right now to talk about the dishes with me?"

☐ Say a little bit and see how the other person is responding. "So that's the first part of what I wanted to tell you. How are you doing so far?"

☐ Be ready and willing to stop. If the other person stops being willing to have the conversation or expresses discomfort, then pause or stop. "I can see this is affecting you more than either of us expected. Should we stop or take a break?"

Now, reimagine your unproductive conversation with some of those consent options included. How would it have improved the outcome of the conversation?

_____

_____

_____

_____

_____

Consent is only the first step. When it comes to attachment, there are two needs: safety and security. Safety is about relief from an experience of threat in the body. Security is about reassurance that connection and resources are and will remain available. When you feel secure with someone, it feels as if that person is there for you and will continue to be there for you and that they see you in a warm, compassionate way. Feeling emotionally safe and secure with someone is the foundation of trust in a relationship.

Until safety and security are adequately present, relationship collaboration (e.g., joint decisions, projects) won't work as well, and healthy communication will be difficult to manage. This exercise will help you explore and identify what it takes for you to feel safe and secure in the midst of a stressful interaction. You might begin by thinking of a specific interaction you had with a relationship partner when your anxious feelings made communication difficult or unproductive.

What can *you* do to soothe your feelings of threat when communication becomes difficult? (Think mainly of things that help your *body* calm down when it is in a state of distress.)

1. _____

2. _____

3. _____

What kinds of things can your partner do to help you soothe feelings of threat? (Again, focus on your body.)

1. _____

2. _____

3. _____

Because difficult communication can activate feelings of insecurity, what can *you* do to soothe your feelings of insecurity and reassure yourself of the relationship connection?

1. _____

2. _____

3. _____

What kinds of things can *your partner* do or say to help reassure you of the relationship connection?

1. _____

2. _____

3. _____

Now, find time to sit down with your partner or loved one, share what you've learned about safety and security, and explore the lists you came up with. The following prompts may guide you through a useful discussion.

- From what you know about me, how effectively do you think the listed items would soothe me?
- Is there anything you'd add to any of these lists?
- Are you willing to help me with any of these things when you recognize that I'm being reactive?

Effective, healthy communication is possible for anxiously attached people, and developing these skills can help you develop and build trust and safety in your close relationships.

Strengthening Your Bonds

It's important to remember that having anxious tendencies doesn't make you a bad person or unworthy of love. You can have a secure relationship regardless of your *individual* insecurity score. *Relationship* security is earned through actions and behaviors that build both partners up and bring out the best in them. Having a high insecurity score just means that you might encounter more challenges.

Appreciation Journal

Appreciation is a wonderful way to build up your relationship capital. You and your partner will feel good spending time acknowledging the ways that you make each other's lives better.

List three things you appreciate about your relationship partner:

1. _____

2. _____

3. _____

List three things you appreciate about yourself:

1. _____

2. _____

3. _____

Taking time to appreciate each other on a regular basis can build goodwill and help ease you through difficult moments. By focusing on appreciation, understanding, and acceptance and by learning healthy communication, anxiously attached individuals can build strong, healthy relationships in which both people feel safe and secure.

Chapter Recap

- Acting out anxious attachment patterns without paying attention to how they affect those around you can burn through your relationship capital.

- People unintentionally act out anxious attachment patterns, because they want to reestablish safety and security in relationship—but these patterns are counterproductive.

- Acceptance and self-compassion are helpful in addressing and supporting yourself or others with anxious attachment. Healthy communication skills is a critical tool that you can learn.

The skills you can learn by working through this chapter include . . .

- Self-compassion for anxious attachment in yourself and empathy for anxious attachment in others

- How to recognize your own limits and respect others' boundaries

- How to diffuse anxious attachment behavior

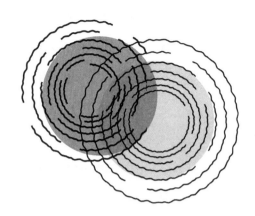

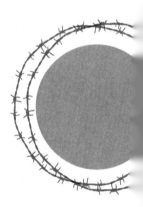

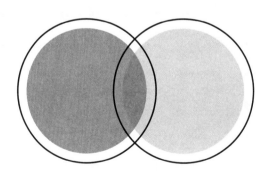

CHAPTER THREE

The Avoidant Attachment Style

If your score on part 2 of the Attachment Quiz (page 14) placed you in the avoidant style, this chapter will help you learn more about what that means and what you can do about it. The higher you scored, the more you're likely to express relationship insecurity through avoidant patterns of behavior. Whereas insecurity comes out as protest and blame in those with an anxious style, the avoidant style minimizes or denies a need for others in the first place. After a presentation of the traits associated with this attachment style, the information and exercises in this chapter will help you develop an awareness of how this style plays out in your relationships (whether you are avoidantly attached or your partner is), learn to accept yourself and others, develop the skills to communicate clearly, and learn how to strengthen your relationship bonds in a way that will leave you feeling more secure.

Traits of the Avoidant Style

Considering your score on the quiz, the higher your insecurity score, the more likely it is that your relationships could be affected negatively by avoidant attachment behaviors. If your insecurity score was low, your relationships may not be as affected.

People with an avoidant attachment style . . .

- Are self-reliant; that is, good at dealing with situations on their own.
- Aren't likely to complain but will show displeasure indirectly.
- Talk about things and ideas, not about themselves.
- Are more likely to report, or be reported as having, memory problems.
- Prefer to deal with conflict in the quickest way possible, even if it means cutting corners.

Avoidance behavior can show up in a variety of ways, like outright ignoring conflict, denying what happened, or escaping discomfort through substances. But it can also be subtler, such as people-pleasing or focusing so much on being helpful to others that you neglect yourself. It can be any response that protects you from feeling ashamed or inadequate.

Here are some examples of people I have come across in my practice who have an avoidant attachment style. As always, the names have been changed.

Kyle has been married for 16 years. Over the past few years, he and his wife have fought more often, with his wife complaining that Kyle doesn't talk about his feelings and gets defensive. Kyle wants to make his wife happy but doesn't know how to change, and he gets stressed when she brings it up over and over.

Dylan has been the peacemaker for his family and friends from age eight, when his parents divorced and it was discovered that he had a talent for listening and helping people feel better. He likes being the peacemaker, because as long as people are complaining to him, they can't be mad at him! He is so good at it that no one ever has an issue with him; they think he is "perfect." Dylan wonders whether people would still love and accept him if he weren't "perfect."

Jee grew up in a strict, fundamentalist Christian family, with little physical affection or emotional connection. She no longer considers herself religious after coming out as a lesbian and being rejected by the church and her parents. Even though she acts aloof about her family's rejection of her, deep down, she longs for their acceptance and can't think about it without getting tearful.

So how do you know if you're playing out an avoidant pattern in your relationships with others? Your relationship partners often tell you that something is getting in the way of their connecting with you, even if it's not readily apparent to you why it's a problem. After enough feedback like this, you might wonder if certain patterns of yours are connected to an unrealistic expectation of self-reliance. This chapter can help you clarify what avoidant attachment behavior looks like and what to do about it.

Self-Awareness

Do you tend to resist depending on people and prefer to keep your distance, even with people who are significant to you? You might have your reasons, but if you have an avoidant style, it boils down to the fact that when you get too close, you feel discomfort, and a type of stress gets activated simply by your becoming dependent on people in practical or emotional ways. Just as with any other form of stress, people create patterns of coping that are not entirely conscious or constructive.

Avoidant attachment in adulthood can take many forms, and the next section describes some patterns that are common for people with the avoidant style. As you read through the description, keep track of how much you identify with, either in the present or in relationships in the past.

HOW AVOIDANT ATTACHMENT FEELS TO YOU

You're fairly self-reliant and proud of that. You probably don't like to talk about yourself very much. You don't chase the spotlight by making your needs known, and it makes you cringe when other people do. Logic and reason are your comfort zones; feelings, not so much. This has served you well in many ways.

Can you think of three specific memories from your childhood when you felt supported, celebrated, or validated by the adults around you? Take as long as you need. Many people can think of warm, joyful, and heartfelt memories with a specific person from childhood. If you can't come up with specific recollections right now, that would go along with an insecure avoidant style. It doesn't mean you don't have fond memories; you just might have fonder ones of being by yourself and entertaining yourself than of being with people. Perhaps you even preferred it that way! Some of the people I've known with strong avoidant tendencies said their fondest memories of childhood involved being by themselves for hours in the woods, daydreaming, or inventing entire plays with stuffed animals in their room.

If you do have memories of your parents showering you with affection, it's likely that in order to get that positive attention, you had to do something "right." They praised or rewarded you for your intelligence, beauty, athleticism, personality, or talent. The message you got was that you were worthy of love and attention when you made the family *look good*.

As an adult, then, it doesn't come naturally to believe that support will be there for you. You're more likely to believe that needing support would inconvenience others, and therefore you can be a better friend, partner, or team/family member by being low maintenance. You train yourself and others to think that you simply don't have needs. You identify with the phrases "I don't need much" and "My needs are simple."

If you're single, you might be interested in a romantic partnership, or want one someday, but you're often unsure because of the potential drawbacks. This leaves you wary about that type of commitment. To test the waters, you might have brief relationships that you end before things get too serious or involved. Breaking up might be uncomfortable, but it's better than feeling trapped later on.

If you're looking for a partner, you might prefer someone who "doesn't take themselves too seriously" or is "easygoing." You value people who aren't too fussy or ask too much of you. If they are too needy, you feel stressed or inadequate and are not likely to keep them around.

If you are already in a committed romantic partnership, you might care a lot for your partner but also need a good amount of distance or "space." If someone gets too close without your invitation, you can feel uncomfortable, even if it isn't rational. Sometimes you may start to feel pressure or stress in a relationship without fully knowing why, and this makes you want to take cover.

As far as your partner's needs and wants, you have a limited tolerance for how much they ask for, even if you can understand intellectually why your partner is asking for it. But in the moment, it just doesn't *seem* necessary. If you have one complaint in your relationship, it's that your partner needs too much from you. When you feel this unwelcome pressure, you seek hobbies, activities, and escapes that are familiar and predictable to you, like work, exercise, porn, or substances.

When you recognize an important desire or need of your own, it can be a lot of work, and even scary, to acknowledge and communicate it to others. It might feel unfamiliar, and you might have little confidence in people to meet your need—which is uncomfortable enough to make you want to forget becoming aware of the need in the first place.

For you, having unmet needs and desires is not the worst thing in the world, as long as you don't focus on them. What gets under your skin is feeling unfairly blamed, condemned, or judged. This hits a particular nerve and can make you want to avoid more, but if you feel unable to escape, you can get uncharacteristically aggressive toward others.

If your score on the insecurity scale was high, your avoidance behavior might take on a more physical form. You might not like hugs or a lot of physical contact in general. Sex might work for you only in specific ways.

Remember that no single description can apply perfectly to anyone, but if your score suggests avoidant attachment, you probably recognized yourself as you read the previous description. When you consider some of your most important experiences in close relationships, how accurate would you rate the description for you?

Not at all
accurate

Completely
accurate

Which parts of that description were most true for you?

_____

_____

_____

_____

_____

_____

_____

_____

_____

Having an avoidant attachment style means that being close to someone can be stressful for you. How do you know if you feel stress simply by being attached to someone? Think of someone you have a significant connection to. Consider if you're sensitive to the person in the following ways:

- You have the subtlest feeling of being trapped when the person comes close or wants to come close to you, either physically or emotionally, because you don't know if you want them that close.
- You become a bit more uncomfortable or irritable when need-ing to shift from doing something by yourself to interacting with the person.
- You're sensitive to detecting when they are about to criticize or blame you.

If some of these resonate with you, you might be experiencing a spike in stress levels as a result of these kinds of interactions. They are inextricably tied to the people you care about and depend on the most, those with whom you probably want to have sustainable, loving, and productive relationships. This stress can throw a wrench in the works in a number of ways.

For example, when you are stressed and need to get something done with the person who stresses you out, you become much more likely to make errors in your thinking and interpretation. You become less attentive toward your partner, you make assumptions that you don't check, and your behavior and signals look evasive or indirectly threatening.

Tyrell and Shannon have been dating for four years. Tyrell feels stressed whenever Shannon is upset. He freezes and can't adequately respond to her requests for comfort. She asks him to reassure her with words or to spend time with her, but even as he is trying, he doubts he's doing it well enough for her. His body tenses and becomes rigid. He can say the words she wants to hear, but his eyes communicate that he isn't really present. Internally, he is scared and anxious about his performance and second-guessing whether those are really the words she wants to hear. In the evenings, when she is likely to be upset from the day or need to talk, he's begun to work more in his office.

Tyrell's brain is working so hard on managing the fear and threat of not doing it right that he isn't able to collaborate in basic ways to help Shannon when she is upset. He knows it looks silly in hindsight, but in the moment, he's helpless to do something about it. Because of how the brain works when it is managing threats, these errors almost always lead in the direction of seeing the other person as more threatening, not less; so it becomes a self-fulfilling prophecy.

Can you imagine being in a situation that demands a lot from you and constantly making errors and being unable to engage fully? You're obviously not at your best. Additionally, if your partner has some version of an insecure attachment, too, then both of you are making a lot of errors in thinking and interpreting each another, causing even more stress for both of you. No wonder you'd rather avoid these situations and retreat to a hobby.

You aren't likely to be the one complaining in relationships, but that isn't always a good thing. Relationships are complicated, and there is rarely a single right answer that needs to be found in a specific moment. However, too much deferred maintenance in a relationship isn't good. The more effective you are at avoiding, the more you might regret it later.

The problem is not about being discerning and prioritizing what you deal with, when you deal with it, and what you put on the back burner. Trouble arises when your avoidant reactions get in the way of getting things done with others or when you don't communicate to your partner what those responses are really about.

Avoidance Inventory

Listed below are emotions and circumstances that come up in relationships that many have reported can feel stressful. Look through the list and identify which ones are stressful for you. Circle all the experiences that make you shy away, withdraw, distract, numb out, and in general feel less connected to the people around you. If you think of others that aren't on the list, write them in the blank spaces.

I'm stressed when I feel . . .

Annoyed	Disappointed	Judged
Anxious	Disgusted	Lonely
Ashamed	Dismissed	Longing/desirous
Betrayed	Envious	Pushed to a limit
Blamed	Guilt ridden	Regretful
Burdened	Helpless	Rejected
Condemning	Humiliated	Resentful
Confused	Hurt	Sad
Contemptuous	Ignored	Self-doubting
Criticized	Inadequate	Stressed
Defeated	Indignant	Unappreciated
Demeaned	Intimidated	Uncomfortable
Devastated	Intolerant	Worried
Diminished	Jealous	_____
_____	_____	_____

I'm stressed when I want/need . . .

Support	Affection/warmth	Appreciation
Safety	Stability	Consistency
Acceptance	To be seen and heard	Fairness/mutuality
Calm/harmony	Joyful connection	To be taken seriously
Structure/order	Security	Relief from duties
_____	_____	_____

It's stressful when the relationship requires . . .

Me to self-disclose	Conflict management	Repair from injury
Me to provide emotional support	Clarifying commitment and agreements	Me to understand my partner
Collaborative decision making	Positive ritual and routine	Managing other relationships
Agreement accountability	Boundary defining	Giving evaluation and/or receiving feedback
_____	_____	_____

I get stressed when I fear . . .

Losing autonomy	Losing free time	Losing my identity
Being replaced	Being abandoned	Being excluded
_____	_____	_____

Nice work! You've just identified the kinds of events that activate your avoidant attachment. Now, go through your selections and list the top three things that cause you to withdraw. You will work with these three specific *triggers* in the next exercise.

Example: It's stressful when the relationship needs conflict management.

1. _____

2. _____

3. _____

Avoidance Pros and Cons

Now, you're going to work with the top three *triggers* for withdrawal or avoidance you identified in the last exercise. Write one trigger at the top of each of the following three tables. Then make a check mark by each reaction you have in response. Finally, you'll explore the ways these behaviors help and hurt your relationships.

1. _____

When this happens, I . . .

☐ Withdraw

☐ Ignore

☐ Distract/stay busy

☐ Numb out/leave

☐ Dismiss myself or others

☐ Deny my experience or others'

☐ Justify/rationalize

☐ Explain something irrelevant

☐ Appease without follow-through

☐ Other: _____

What do I gain by doing these things?

_____

_____

What do I miss out on by doing these things?

_____

_____

What is a more constructive response to this trigger?

_____

_____

2. _____

When this happens, I . . .

- ☐ Withdraw
- ☐ Ignore
- ☐ Distract/stay busy
- ☐ Numb out/leave
- ☐ Dismiss myself or others
- ☐ Deny my experience or others'
- ☐ Justify/rationalize
- ☐ Explain something irrelevant
- ☐ Appease without follow-through
- ☐ Other: _____

What do I gain by doing these things?

_____

_____

What do I miss out on by doing these things?

_____

_____

What is a more constructive response to this trigger?

_____

_____

3. _____

When this happens, I . . .

☐ Withdraw

☐ Ignore

☐ Distract/stay busy

☐ Numb out/leave

☐ Dismiss myself or others

☐ Deny my experience or others'

☐ Justify/rationalize

☐ Explain something irrelevant

☐ Appease without follow-through

☐ Other: _____

What do I gain by doing these things?

_____

_____

What do I miss out on by doing these things?

_____

_____

What is a more constructive response to this trigger?

_____

_____

Remember that all of these behaviors were learned. None of them is your fault, but the consequences of these behaviors *are* your business. If you're satisfied with how these reactions are working for you, then carry on! If you're no longer okay with the results, it's in your power to change the behaviors that cause them.

Awareness of Others

Perhaps it's not your tendency to display these avoidant behaviors, but you're in a relationship with someone who does. This section will help you understand and respond to them effectively when this happens.

HOW IT FEELS WHEN OTHERS ARE AVOIDANTLY ATTACHED

When people play out avoidant attachment patterns, it can feel as if they're leaving a vacuum where their involvement or support is desired or expected. Top complaints about people with avoidant attachment patterns are that they:

- Don't want to deal with problems.
- Have commitment issues.
- Are not in touch with their feelings.
- "Check out" or withdraw.
- Are filtered, guarded, or rejecting.
- Do things without telling you.

Eventually, these patterns can make it feel as if your avoidant friend, family member, or partner doesn't care about you.

So, what can you do about that? Sometimes you need to remind yourself that it simply isn't true. People with avoidant attachment have trouble feeling at ease in attachment relationships, and unless you knew them when they were babies, it has been true long before you met them. There are just things that are stressful for them, and it's not personal.

The Effect on You

Think of a time you needed help or support from someone specific, and they either were absent or were there but didn't feel entirely present.

What was the incident?

_____

_____

_____

What do you remember feeling?

_____

_____

_____

What thoughts do you remember having?

_____

_____

_____

How did your body hold that experience?

_____

_____

_____

For people with avoidant attachment, relying on someone too much can evoke panic and discomfort. For them, this discomfort can range from just a bit of stress to a full-blown threat response. Many types of interpersonal engagement, especially of an intense nature, can set off avoidant tendencies. As a friend, partner, collaborator, or family member of someone who gets triggered in this way, what can you do? In the previous exercise, you may have noted your own difficult reactions to their responses.

The first thing is to take the person's need for safety and comfort seriously. Taking the risk to engage in emotionally charged situations, even if they may seem simple to *you*, is not easy for people with *avoidant attachment*. For them, staying engaged in the conversation about an emotionally charged topic could be the hardest thing they do all week.

Helping your partner feel safer may also help you get what you want. Conversations and projects that are important to you will go better if the avoidant person has a chance to feel safe while engaged. When people's systems are managing threat, their brains are not going to do the complex tasks as well—the tasks that are typically needed for effective collaboration.

We can't read other people's minds when it comes to what is safe for them, but it is almost always possible to read when something isn't right, if we know where to look. For all of us, regardless of attachment style, there is a concept called *window of tolerance*, which describes the ideal zone of physiological activation that allows a person to function most effectively. When someone shows physical signs that they are outside this zone, either with too-high or too-low arousal, this is usually an indication that their body is interpreting some kind of danger, real or imagined. Since people who form avoidant attachments are unlikely to verbalize their distress, understanding this concept can be very useful.

Your best chance of success lies in both of you staying in the window of tolerance when having difficult conversations. When having an emotionally charged conversation with someone with avoidant attachment, these tips can help:

- Establish friendly rapport. Don't just assume that your partner knows you mean well. Use touch or eye contact from the beginning to establish it clearly, but in a nonthreatening way.
- Timing is everything. It's better to get something done and celebrate a small victory, taking up the rest another time, than to try to do everything in a sitting and push yourself or others beyond their window of tolerance.
- Learn to read your partner's face, eyes, and body language and know when they have had too much. Once you learn to understand someone's window of tolerance, distress cues can be clear. Too-high arousal can look like talking faster or in a more frantic manner, a deer-in-the-headlights look, rapid breathing, or trembling or shaking. Too-low arousal can manifest as dimming of the eyes, appearing numb or vacant, slurred or slow speech, collapsed posture, and getting very cold all of a sudden.
- Be willing to slow down when you see your partner leave the window of tolerance. If possible, establish ahead of time what might provide relief. Some people just need a friendly smile and a pause before moving forward. Others could use reassurance, like, "You're doing great. We can take our time." Some would welcome having their hand held or other contact that feels good.

At this point you may think, "Hey, this is a lot of work!" You would be right. People sometimes require going the extra mile. At the same time, with experience and practice, it does get easier. Doing anything worthwhile takes knowledge and practice, and your relationships are no exception.

Last, don't forget to be aware of *yourself*. Look at the earlier exercise to see how you react to avoidance or distancing behaviors. Are you hurt, angry, critical, resentful, or condemning? If your reaction is strong, you may need to take a step back and take care of yourself. Reach out to offer support only if you have enough for yourself or can feel replenished by giving to the relationship.

Working with a Negative Reaction

If you often find yourself frustrated by people who withdraw, this exercise is for you. Think of the last time you had a negative reaction to someone who was withdrawn when you needed them. What shape did your body want to make? Did your shoulders tense up? Did your chest puff out? Did your stomach feel tight? Did you ball up your fists? Maybe some combination?

Now, with your entire body, re-create the shape that you remember in a more exaggerated fashion and hold the shape for three breaths. For example, if you remember your neck craning out, your jaw tightening, and your fists balling up, go ahead and do these three things together and hold this position tightly for three breaths. During these three breaths, think of something you might think or believe in that moment, like, "My partner doesn't care." On the third exhale, release everything all at once—relaxing your neck, jaw, and fists—and let your mind empty. Notice what thoughts you have when you let everything relax.

Now repeat the same sequence two more times, thinking of the same negative reaction.

When you're done, jot down some notes about what you experienced:

_____

_____

_____

Upon doing the exercise the second and third times, was the negative response more intense, less intense, or the same? Why do you think this was?

_____

_____

_____

Learning Acceptance

As we discussed in chapter 2, acceptance is about being open to events in the present and past without trying to change them. When we practice acceptance, we can develop the capacity to give up the battle that we often have with reality. Instead, we can take responsibility for our experience and actions when possible and make choices that align better with our values. As with most things, it begins with ourselves.

ACCEPTING YOURSELF

Sometimes, thinking about the unhelpful traits you learned as a child might cause you to self-criticize and compare yourself with others. "Well, my sister had the same parents, and she doesn't seem to be avoidant, like I am." First of all, comparisons like this are usually inaccurate, because you don't know the full story of other people's relationships. Second, they create unnecessary pressure and stress that can exacerbate the problems you're already struggling with. It ends up being a negative cycle.

Instead, try forgiving yourself for the past and accepting yourself for the feelings and thoughts that are so automatic and ingrained that you can't change the fact that you have them. Accepting the different aspects of yourself with warmth and care is the most important thing you can get from this book.

Exploring the Avoidant Inner Child

The following prompt will take you on a brief journey of imagination where you will have the opportunity to feel empathy for the very early experiences that encouraged avoidant attachment behavior. Allow yourself to imagine the feelings and body sensations of the child.

Imagine you are a baby. You've just been fed, and your mother puts you back into your crib. As you transition from her warm embrace to the cold bed and watch her face vanish, you start to feel frightened. You don't know where she's going and whether she's coming back. You feel unprotected and unsafe. You tense up and cry, wanting her to come back. Not seeing her, you cry even louder, hoping that will make a difference, but it doesn't.

Your mom is ignoring your cries. It's not in a mean way—she knows that you are fed and dry and warm, so what more could you want? You're safe, and it's time for you to go to sleep. You'll figure out how on your own.

Eventually, what you figure out is that no one is coming when you feel scared, so you stop crying because it's no use. Instead, you soothe yourself, suck your thumb, and look at the blurry world around you as you rock yourself to sleep. This will get you through until the next feeding time. Sadly, here in this crib, you just learned that others can simply ignore your instinctive need for essential connection, and you can, too.

As you grow into a child, you have many more experiences of spending time alone: playing alone, imagining alone, and taking care of needs on your own. These are the times you feel safest. Being alone is the home base you go to when you feel bothered by the world. Growing older means learning new ways to be alone, through reading, video games, art, and other activities. You can create entire worlds that exist just in your mind without having to really interact with anyone else. Others can disappoint you, but being alone never will.

What feelings did you imagine and empathize with while reading the passage above?

_____

_____

_____

What words of empathy do you have for the child in the passage?

_____

_____

_____

Speaking directly to the child in the passage, what encouraging advice do you have?

_____

_____

_____

ACCEPTING OTHERS

Maintaining a relationship with someone with an avoidant attachment style presents challenges. The person can be difficult to read, indirect with communication, and absent when you need them. Accepting people isn't about condoning their behavior or even tolerating it when it affects you negatively. It's about acknowledging their actions and behavior without imposing your wish for them to be different. Just as with self-acceptance, accepting others creates a nonjudgmental space that welcomes curiosity and change.

Empathy in Action

This exercise can be helpful when you're faced with avoidant behavior that leaves you feeling disappointed or let down. Think of a specific time in your life when someone important felt absent or less engaged when you needed them. Pick an incident that isn't too activating in the present moment.

A time someone important to me left me feeling alone was . . .

_____

_____

_____

Instead of what they did, I wanted them to . . .

_____

_____

_____

The situation was stressful for them, because they have a difficult time with . . .

_____

_____

_____

I know this is stressful for them, because . . .

_____

_____

_____

They judged themselves or believed that I judged them as _____. But in reality, they are still learning how to _____, and they are not always perfect at it. When they get overwhelmed, they can _____. They react from reflex instead and forget how much I need them.

You might practice this with a number of incidents; with practice, you'll develop an approach to dealing with these incidents in real time, and you may also develop a greater understanding of and empathy for your avoidant partner.

Healthy Communication

Most avoidantly attached people are uncomfortable with conflict and shy away from managing it. They feel anxiety and stress when conflict is present and respond by avoiding it in some way. Some simply do not know how to adequately represent themselves when it comes to staking a position. They rely on ideas and external authority to make their point instead of sharing personally. But even when avoidantly attached people know exactly where they stand and what they want, they may still give up before the task is done, because staying assertive and collaborative at the same time can feel intense and overwhelming.

In my practice, I often witness people feeling intimidated by and even terrified of conflict. One approach that helps is when partners stay "on task," with only one topic getting addressed at a time. I highly recommend you and your partner adopt this agreement as the two of you consider your ground rules for dealing with conflict. Oh, did I mention that it's a good idea to establish ground rules? It is!

LaRhonda and Maree had been in counseling with me for several months. They had divergent insecure styles, with LaRhonda being avoidant and Maree being more anxious. When they fought, Maree's anxiety often overpowered the interaction, leaving LaRhonda feeling as if she had to catch up and defend herself until she got overwhelmed and gave up. LaRhonda felt resentful, and

Maree wondered why she didn't feel the connection or support she longed for. They recognized that this wasn't sustainable and agreed to try keeping their conversations to one topic. This is how it played out in a counseling session shortly after:

"I think the house could be neater," said LaRhonda.

"You don't think I make an effort to keep it neat?" asked Maree.

A few months earlier, LaRhonda would have taken this as a cue that Maree would not be open to her views. But because LaRhonda had been working on staying engaged in her part of conflicts, she continued, "I know you do. This isn't about one or the other of us being the cause of the mess. I know I forget, too. I would like to live in a cleaner house."

Maree responded, "Okay. I can make more effort, but I don't think you realize how careless you are with the dishes on the counter and leaving your work stuff everywhere."

Again, LaRhonda would have previously felt blamed, lost steam in the argument, and then despaired. She took a deep breath and forged on. "Would you like to know what would make me happy?" She paused and waited for a response.

"Yes. What's that?"

With great effort, LaRhonda said, "I would really like for our living room and kitchen to be tidied up midweek, before the weekend, when we do our deep cleaning. I think that would make a big difference."

"My issue is that I'm often out with my friends and don't know when I'll be home midweek," Maree replied. "You go out with your friends a lot more on the weekend, and sometimes I'm wondering whether I'll even see you over the weekend. And when I do, you're playing video games."

At this point, Maree's focus shifted away from the topic of tidying up to a familiar complaint: She doesn't feel she gets enough time with LaRhonda.

If LaRhonda hadn't said something to corral them back, I would've, because I didn't want them to lose their forward momentum. But I didn't have to.

> *"We can talk about my video game playing another time, sweetie. Right now, we're talking about cleaning the house. So, what do you think of my idea of building in a way to clean the living room and kitchen midweek so we don't have to live with a messy house until the weekend?"*

> *"Oh, okay. I can live with that. We just have to figure out the details."*

They both made it to the finish line.

Changing relationship patterns sometimes takes perseverance. At each juncture, LaRhonda took control to steer the conversation. She kept it focused and collaborative, and made sure her avoidant patterns did not stop her. LaRhonda didn't develop these skills overnight, but she knew that the relationship couldn't handle the same fights over and over. With time, she found confidence to bring things forward. It helped that she saw Maree also making an effort to be less reactive and more receptive to her own attempts to speak up.

In this example, LaRhonda did a good job of reorienting the conversation each time it veered off course. This is a multifaceted skill, but LaRhonda had to begin somewhere. The first thing she did was become more aware of her own strong preference for order in the home.

Now, explore an issue that you don't feel totally fulfilled by in a specific relationship. If nothing comes to mind that strongly, just make a best guess. The point is to explore your thoughts and desires as they relate to that particular relationship.

When I think about this relationship, the thing I don't feel satisfied by is . . .

_____

_____

_____

_____

What would make me happy is . . .

_____

_____

_____

_____

If I got what I wanted, I would feel . . .

_____

_____

_____

_____

How will it affect my relationship in the long term if I never advocate for myself on this issue?

_____

_____

_____

_____

RATING SCALE: *How much effort am I willing to make to assert myself on this issue? (Circle)*

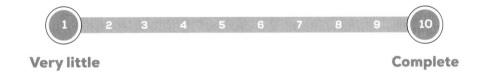

Very little   **Complete**

LaRhonda didn't give up when the conversation started to frustrate her. After learning about Maree's attachment style, she knew that Maree wasn't trying to blame her or change the focus of the conversation on purpose. LaRhonda knew that stress from attachment conditioning can affect people differently and sometimes makes conversation less orderly and more chaotic. She also remembered that she and Maree had agreed to try to engage in conflict with one another in a more orderly way to reduce the chance that the conversation would get derailed and the two of them would have a difficult evening together.

Instead of giving up when she heard criticism and blame from Maree, LaRhonda said the following things:

"I know you do, but it isn't about one or the other of us being the cause of the mess. I know I forget, too. I would like to live in a cleaner house."

"Would you like to know what would make me happy? . . . I would really like for our living room and kitchen to be tidied up midweek, before the weekend, when we do our deep cleaning. I think that would make a big difference."

"We can talk about my video game playing another time, sweetie. Right now we're talking about cleaning the house. So what do you think of my idea of building in a way to clean the living room and kitchen midweek so that we don't have to live with a messy house until the weekend?"

Advocating for an Issue

In this exercise, you're going to practice advocating for the issue you wrote about in the previous exercise. Your goal for the conversation is to . . .

- Stick with one topic.
- Keep it focused.
- Communicate respect and reassurance.
- Find an agreement that works for both of you.

Think of responses you would have to these common communication challenges.

Your partner feels attacked and blames you:

_____

_____

_____

_____

_____

Your partner brings up the past and, again, seems to blame you:

_____

_____

_____

_____

_____

Your partner launches a countercomplaint about a completely different topic:

_____

_____

_____

_____

_____

Developing the skills to find a healthy way of communicating, whether you are avoidant or your partner is, takes time and effort, but your relationship will benefit. You may have to take deep breaths and persist, as LaRhonda did, but doing so will eventually get easier.

Strengthening Your Bonds

We attach to people in order to feel tethered in the world to someone safe and comforting. Some of those bonds are primary lifelines we depend on. When it comes to strengthening those connections so you can more fully enjoy your relationships, it's important to manage the attachment stress that can bubble up. The following exercise will help you think about your attachment stress, as well as that of your partner. Being more conscious of these stresses is one step toward navigating them together.

Perspective Matrix

David got engaged to Vasna last year, and David's avoidant attachment tendencies have shown up in the wedding-planning process. Vasna has been extremely eager to plan the wedding. David agreed numerous times to sit down and help with the planning because he thought he should; but he hasn't actually made the time. He doesn't really like planning and isn't sure what kind of wedding he wants or can afford. To soothe his anxiety about money, he's been working more hours but has said very little to Vasna about it. Vasna is becoming more impatient by the day and has started to feel hurt that David is not serious about the wedding.

Situations like this often cause conflict because of an inadequate understanding of how the avoidantly attached partner is experiencing stress. Below is an exercise you might use to capture these nuances, whether the person with avoidant behavior is you or your partner. Here is an example matrix, inspired by David's avoidant behavior.

Name	How was the situation experienced?	What is stressful (considering attachment style)?	How stressful? (1–10)
David	I'm stressed out about money, and I'm taking care of the situation by working more hours to save for the wedding. Vasna doesn't seem too concerned about money, so I don't think I'll really be understood.	Stress about money	5 Moderate
		Fear that I'll disappoint Vasna	9 Very high
		Not being good at planning	7 High

Even though David had a variety of stressors (from moderate to very highly stressful), he didn't directly communicate any of them to Vasna, nor was she aware of them. A conversation clarifying these stressors might help them both understand what was at stake.

Now, create your own perspective matrix around a situation that brought out avoidant behavior in yourself or a partner:

Name	How was the situation experienced?	What is stressful (considering attachment style)?	How stressful? (1–10)

This is an exercise that you can come back to when you or someone you care about is acting out of avoidance. This worksheet can help you see if you are both on the same page about your stressors.

Chapter Recap

- Avoidant attachment happens when the mere act of attaching (dependence) makes someone prone to stress in a way that activates behaviors and patterns that tend to be dismissive or avoidant.

- When it comes to responding to avoidant attachment, it is more effective to consider safety and stress relief before solutions.

The skills you can learn by working through this chapter include . . .

- How to bring up an issue for discussion and keep the conversation on task

- How to identify the specific experiences that trigger an avoidant response using the Avoidance Inventory (page 57)

- How to recognize when your partner is outside their window of tolerance and what to do about it

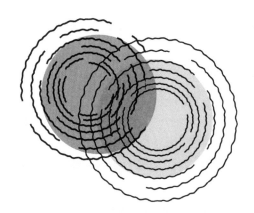

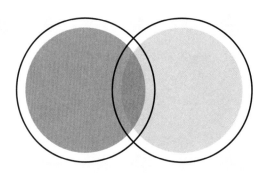

CHAPTER FOUR

The Secure Attachment Style

Finally, we've arrived at the secure style of attachment, the model of relationship health we all strive for. People who have this style, or develop it, aren't prone to experiencing extra stress when it comes to attaching to, and depending on, people close to them. Even if your score didn't put you in this category, this chapter will be a guide to what is possible.

Traits of the Secure Style

People with a secure attachment style . . .

- Are able to easily make adjustments to new information and changing circumstances.
- Feel hopeful about and prioritize relationships.
- Value repair when there has been an injury or breach in a relationship.
- Handle differences and complexity in relationships with confidence.

Being securely attached allows you to think and process in a clear way, even when things are complex or you're in conflict. Your nervous system doesn't get stressed out about being close to people, which frees you from needing to defend against unwanted anxiety triggered by closeness and intimacy. This allows you to focus on solving problems with your romantic partner, family member, or close friend. Bonding with others, a universal human need, is overall a smoother and more enjoyable experience.

Here are some examples of people in my practice who have a predominantly secure attachment style:

Tilda had encountered an onslaught of tragedy and bad luck last year. She got laid off from work, and her mother passed away from cancer. Months later, she and her husband lost their house to wildfire. She credits her relationship with her husband for providing stability throughout the waves of terrible news. "It was hard for both of us, but we knew that we would eventually get through it," Tilda told me. "I don't know what I would've done without him."

Ayanna is a software engineer who loves her work and has developed a fantastic working relationship with her team. When friends on the team asked her to join their risky move to start a new company, she thought about it for some time because she was typically risk averse. It wasn't an easy decision, but she agreed because she valued the relationships and believed in their ability to continue building new and exciting projects together.

Harvey works 48-hour shifts as a firefighter. When he gets to the firehouse, he is ready every time to entrust his life to his fellow first responders and is committed to doing everything in his power to not let anyone down.

Secure attachment doesn't make people immune to relationship problems. People with secure attachment can make the same relationship mistakes and have to learn the same lessons as everyone else. They can get involved with people who aren't good for them, fail to manage conflict well in a relationship, be avoidant or reactive, and so on. But securely attached people tend to bounce back faster and more fully from disappointments, and they learn from these experiences to avoid repeating them if they can. In other words, securely attached people show more resilience in their relationships.

How do they do it? Remember that *attachment security* is the sense that when we associate with people in the most intimate of ways, emotionally and physically, these people are going to do their best for us—they won't betray or abandon us. Through their experiences, secure people learned that it is possible to trust and rely on others. Generally, they had the benefit of being well cared for from a young age. And when they had negative experiences, they had someone to help them through it. This kind of early formative experience helps them feel at ease about relationships.

Self-Awareness

As with any other attachment style, securely attached people come in all sizes, shapes, backgrounds, and personalities. Securely attached people experience the full range of highs and lows, just like anyone else in a relationship, and their self-awareness is an important process of learning. Your relationships can always benefit from more awareness about how your thoughts, feelings, and body sensations affect what you do with others and how it impacts them.

If you scored low on insecurity and high on security on the Attachment Quiz (page 9), chances are good that you will recognize yourself in the following description. If there are parts that don't speak to you, know that the idea of perfect secure attachment is aspirational, reflecting a general idea, rather than any specific person at a point in time. Finally, the most important aspects of the secure style can be learned through awareness and development.

HOW SECURE ATTACHMENT FEELS TO YOU

The relationships you value, you value very much. You get a lot out of them, even when things aren't perfect, in part because you accept that no relationship is perfect. What is important is that these relationships give you strength daily and when there's a crisis.

You're pretty flexible when it comes to your relationships. You're sensitive to your own and others' needs and wants. If you do have a bias, at times you might be too accommodating, but not often to the point of completely sacrificing your own needs. If you have done that in the past, then you've learned from that mistake.

You're comfortable with having certain needs, and you can communicate them and make requests. If the other person can't meet your need, it might be a little disappointing, but you move on. You figure out how that need could be met elsewhere. You know you weren't wrong for asking and that your need is valid.

When there's a problem, you tend to focus on the problem itself rather than the people involved. While you can acknowledge that people have faults, yourself included, finger-pointing doesn't seem productive. We are all who we are. You seek help when a problem really stumps you.

If you find out that you've hurt someone you care about, you try your best to repair it. You can consistently do this without getting defensive or giving up, because you're aware that you can affect others in negative ways, even when you mean well. Conversely, when you've been deeply hurt, you give the other person a chance to repair things with you. You don't hold grudges.

Your approach to romantic partnership is fairly relaxed. Finding someone right away who is right for you would be great, but if it takes a while, that's okay by you, too. When you find someone you're interested in, you tend to take your time getting to know the person. Even if you're head-over-heels in love, you can still do the mental math of how compatible you are long term and let that factor into your dating decisions. You think about the future and plan for it, but you don't stress too much about the nuts and bolts or dwell on the past when things get challenging.

In a relationship with someone, you move toward shared positive goals and visions together, rather than holding a zero-sum understanding of relationships that allows only one person to get what they want at once.

While there is no single factor that predicts a secure attachment style, there are early conditions that encourage it. You likely felt valued and seen by one or both parents. And beyond that, you may have also had the support of teachers, friends, and family members who encouraged and appreciated you. Whether at home or somewhere else, you had a guiding figure who gave you solace and comfort when you needed it and served as a safe home base from which to explore the complexity of the world. This in turn gave you confidence that things in your life would work out, one way or another. It's not blind faith; your approach to life and relationships allows you to see them as an evolving, unfolding process. There is always something new to be gained and to discover.

Skills for Promoting Secure Relationships

Developing better relationship skills is a process. The more work you put in, the better you'll get. Take a moment here to take inventory of the things you do well and the things you'd like to improve. (You can do this even if you have an *insecure* attachment style!)

For each item, put a check mark by the things you already do well and a plus symbol for skills you want to improve.

- ☐ Detecting when people I care about are not being entirely honest
- ☐ Detecting early on when people I care about are upset in a conversation
- ☐ Keeping a conversation on topic during conflict
- ☐ Staying appreciative of my loved ones and communicating it to them
- ☐ Soothing my partner
- ☐ Knowing my own boundaries with time, emotional energy, or physical comfort/safety
- ☐ Communicating my feelings, needs, or desires
- ☐ Taking the lead in a relationship
- ☐ Collaborating for a win-win
- ☐ De-escalating stressful interactions
- ☐ Showing appreciation and gratitude

Each of these is an important skill for promoting security in close relationships. Take stock of the items you already do well, and give yourself a pat on the back!

Now, for the items you want to work on, what are ways you can think of to improve? If you can't think of anything, consult a friend you respect and ask for suggestions.

_____

_____

_____

_____

_____

_____

What are some ways I can improve in the areas I want to develop?

Example: I can watch a documentary or educational video about deception to get better at telling when people aren't being truthful. I might take an improv class to learn how to take the lead and collaborate better on a win-win solution.

_____

_____

_____

_____

_____

_____

Just as people with insecure attachment don't *always* behave insecurely in relationships, people who attach securely don't behave securely at all times. But when they do behave insecurely and conflict arises, things go a lot more smoothly and get back on track faster.

People who respond in securely attached ways are generally even-keeled and oriented in the present. They don't worry too much about the future or dwell on the past. They deal with what needs to be addressed in the present—which is harder than it sounds! When someone disagrees with them, they can make a good argument without putting the other person down.

They are collaborative in the truest sense. They value fairness and don't sacrifice others' needs for theirs or vice versa. They strive to be fair and allow others to say exactly what they need to say.

It can be a tremendous gift when securely attached people trust their instincts and are skillful enough to lead during moments of stress. Because their nervous system tends to be more even-keeled, if someone is upset with them, it doesn't trigger feelings of abandonment, which would make them react, or engulfment, which would make them avoid.

Awareness of Others

It's important not to pigeonhole *anyone* based on a fixed idea of their attachment style. People who operate from secure attachment tend toward responses that are fairer and more collaborative, but anyone can respond this way, regardless of attachment style. Thus, it's more important to be able to recognize *behaviors* that are secure-functioning behaviors rather than make assumptions based on a label. Being able to recognize secure attachment will help you identify a productive path to getting something done in the relationship.

Being in relationship with someone who is securely attached can feel like this: Imagine you are learning to juggle with someone. You juggle the balls back and forth and learn tricks. Sometimes you can keep the balls in the air for a while, and other times they fall. It's all a learning experience. Your juggling partner is doing the same and is more or less dependable. When the balls drop, they pick them up and put them back in play. Your partner's participation feels as if it makes you both better, and it's *fun*.

To recognize secure attachment, you also need to know how to recognize behaviors that are easily mistaken for secure but are concealing insecurity— what Stan Tatkin calls *pseudosecure*. Pseudosecure traits can cause confusion when one is first getting to know the ins and outs of the secure attachment style. Below is a list of relationship dynamics and traits that can sometimes masquerade as secure behavior, along with suggestions for responding to them productively. Again, remember that the idea of secure attachment here is aspirational! There is always room to evolve and grow.

Pseudosecure traits:

- Always or frequently accommodating what you want. A relationship is about two people. If someone says they agree with you even when you suspect they don't, at least not entirely, this is not secure. If you're not sure, ask them why they are agreeing, and look for real evidence that they're getting something worthwhile, too.

- Being perfect on paper or social media. A partner, or relationship, can look good when content is selectively shared and, sometimes, staged. These staged scenes give you zero information about how someone actually behaves under stress with others. Try not to believe assumptions that you don't have evidence to support.

- Countering with a complaint about you, when you bring up a concern or grievance, because "it's only fair." If they counter with an unrelated topic, that usually means they weren't really able to tolerate your feedback. If this happens, ask the other person if they can agree to stay on topic about your issue, provided you are willing to revisit *their* complaint later.

- Always being there to support you but seeming not to have any problems or to need support. If this is a relationship in which you would value mutual support, consider why they don't show their needs in the relationship. Does this dynamic affect your relationship in negative ways? Does it set you up to always feel like the mess who needs to be rescued? Does it result in your feeling as if you are too much of a burden and they are not? Consider whether this really works for you.

- Claiming that they should be able to do what they want in a relationship because they don't want to be controlled. Yes, people should be free to make choices, but they also have to accept that what they do affects others. If this happens, make sure you are clear with yourself about what boundaries keep you safe and feeling comfortable in your own skin. Remember, you get to decide what is and isn't workable for you.

- Insisting on dealing with certain issues because they feel anxious, even if it overwhelms you or it just isn't the right time. Conflict management is necessary but isn't always fun, and sometimes it raises some difficult emotions. But it's not considered secure to bypass your extreme discomfort and compel you to do something you don't feel ready for. If this happens, ask for time and let them know the conditions that would help you discuss a topic productively. Do you want to talk in person? In writing? Can you discuss it only for an hour?

- Not getting upset but being critical of you for getting upset. When people are secure, they don't tend to blame anything on how *you* feel. If this happens, try to be curious about why they're trying to put the blame on you. Ask if difficult feelings, like anger, make them uncomfortable.

- Telling you that your relationship skills aren't up to par. Using shame or judgment is a primitive way of exerting influence over another person. It's not the same as accountability, where the agreements are clearly defined and people can separate the action from the person. If this happens, take a step back and remember what your goals are for the relationship. Then you can decide whether to try to redirect the conversation to something more productive or to respond in another way.

Recognizing secure attachment is nuanced, and it can take a while to fully comprehend. As a general rule, though, secure attachment behavior in relationships makes room for more than one person to feel good, be right, and get their needs met. If one person is getting one or more of these things at the expense of the other, then this is not secure attachment.

Continuing to explore the nuances of secure attachment, secure and insecure approaches can look the same if you don't know what thoughts and feelings motivated the person to make the decision. Imagine this:

Two of your male friends, Dru and Arron, are in long-term relationships with female partners. They tell you that they agreed to make a big concession to their partners and give up on the opportunity to become a parent, despite both having told you previously that they wanted children. The difference is, Dru does so from a secure attachment orientation, while Arron does so from an insecure attachment orientation.

After Dru tries at length to understand his partner Kari's position and explain his, he accepts that they each want different things, both for valid reasons. He knows that Kari isn't backing down. He feels sad when he thinks about the prospect of either losing Kari or losing his opportunity to be a father; but he imagines being able to be happy without children, while he finds it hard to imagine being as happy without Kari. This leads him to offer a concession, on the condition that they stay involved in the lives of their nieces and nephews. After they agree, Dru is glad to put the issue behind them so they can make the most of their mostly kid-free lives together.

Arron and his partner, Wilma, have argued about kids over the past two years, and he is exhausted. Wilma won't budge. He doesn't want to lose the relationship and feels paralyzed about what to do next. If he stops bringing it up, then they don't have to fight about it again; so Arron accepts defeat and tells Wilma he's not going to push anymore. When he thinks about his decision, Arron feels more than a twinge of resentment and senses that perhaps he is willing to make more sacrifices for the relationship than Wilma is.

Even though Dru and Arron both made the decision to give up the opportunity to be a father in order to make their relationships work, they did so with different motivations. As a result, they experienced different outcomes. To really understand someone's attachment style, you can't just look at actions alone. You have to understand the person's motivations, feelings, and thoughts.

In a challenging situation, like dealing with a partner who wants to share a life together while wanting very different things, operating from a secure foundation will allow for greater clarity in the face of complexity.

Secure versus Insecure Approach

As we saw with Dru and Arron, the same basic outcome might occur whether you are securely or insecurely attached, but the internal experience of feelings and thoughts—before, during, and after the decision—can be very different.

In this exercise, you'll have a chance to pick a decision you've made within a relationship and explore the reasons for making the decision based on secure attachment or insecure attachment. For example, this worksheet describes Dru's and Arron's decisions to give up fatherhood:

Decision: Making a big concession and agreeing to not have children, even though fatherhood was a dream	
Insecure approach (Arron):	**Secure approach (Dru):**
1. Feels scared about losing the relationship. 2. Feels somewhat paralyzed with indecision. Default is inaction and not having kids. 3. Doesn't want to create more conflict, which will make them both upset, so the concession makes sense. 4. Is left with feelings of resentment and defeat.	1. Feels sad about both the prospect of losing his partner and losing his opportunity to be a father. 2. Can imagine being happy without kids, deciding it is better than being without his much-valued partner. 3. Makes the concession and asks for something in return. 4. Feels relieved that he made a decision and is able to move on.

Now, it's your turn. Fill out your own worksheet, beginning with a decision that you've already made pertaining to a relationship. Then put your thoughts and feelings about the decision in the appropriate column, Secure or Insecure. Next, fill out thoughts and feelings that would fit the other category, even if they are hypothetical. The point is to practice identifying whether thoughts and feelings emerge from a secure or an insecure place.

Decision	
My Decision is:	
Insecure approach:	Secure approach:

Questions to consider:

1. What conditions help you have a secure approach to a relationship?
2. What conditions promote an insecure approach?

HOW TO RESPOND TO SECURE ATTACHMENT

If you recognize secure attachment in a relationship, it most likely feels as if the other person collaborates with you to get the best outcome possible. The best way to respond is by bringing your own willingness to collaborate in mutually satisfying ways. When two people do this, there is great potential for getting things done.

This, of course, means clarifying your needs, desires, and stance on the topic at hand, to the best of your ability. Try to understand the other person's respective needs and desires, as well.

When there is conflict, understand your common goals. If you are romantic partners, you might want to reinforce and strengthen your relationship in the face of new challenges. If you are business partners, your goal might be to clarify what values are important for your new venture. If you are parent and adult child, your goal might be to discover a relationship as friends and equals.

If anything gets in the way of collaboration on common goals, address it first. It might be other relationships, responsibilities, or personal deficits.

Imagine a Secure Interaction with Conflict

Most of us get so caught up in the fast pace of conflict that we sometimes don't notice when the other person is offering an olive branch. When these moments are missed, fights last longer and are more stressful.

Recall a time when you were involved with a difficult relationship conflict that didn't go so well, and the other person reacted out of fear or hurt. Remember what this was like—the feelings, thoughts, and body sensations that you experienced in response.

What did the other person do that triggered your reaction?

_____

_____

_____

_____

Now, imagine that the other person can think and feel beyond themself, instead of just being scared or hurt, and can make an effort to really see your perspective, as well. Imagine the other person as their most generous and compassionate self. The person speaks to you calmly and looks at you with a warm sparkle in their eye. What do you feel now?

_____

_____

_____

_____

You probably felt better. This is what happens when we feel that the person we care about can consider us. If so, really let that good feeling in. Now, imagine showing appreciation for the different response. How would you show your appreciation and encourage the other person to keep doing what you see and hear them doing? (Example: I would give them a hug, I would thank them and tell them things I think they are right about.)

Learning Acceptance

Accepting reality is necessary for healthy relationships, whether this means accepting what your partner thinks and feels, understanding that you have disappointed one another, or perhaps accepting external circumstances that affect your relationship. If relationship processes were a recipe, acceptance would be gathering the necessary ingredients. If you omitted ingredients or made inappropriate substitutes, no matter how hard you tried, the recipe might not come out as intended.

ACCEPTING YOURSELF

As always, begin with yourself. How often do you acknowledge where you are and the aspects of yourself that are less than perfect? Accepting yourself means making space for something to be *as it is*, to make peace with it so you don't spend precious energy and resources trying to fight it. This goes for body sensations, thoughts and feelings, and actions that have already happened. These arise and pass. We don't always have control over them, nor do we have to.

Accepting Yourself as Perfectly Imperfect

In what areas of the relationship do you expect perfection from yourself or get self-critical when you don't do well? (Example: I'm very hard on myself when I make my partner upset.)

_____

_____

How do you feel when you criticize yourself? (Example: I feel deflated.)

_____

_____

What do you do when you feel this way? (Example: I binge eat.)

_____

_____

Excessive self-criticism is rarely a useful way to change or encourage new behaviors. Recognizing how harsh you can be to yourself, take a moment to notice the part of you that pays the price. Is it your body and physical health? Is it your self-esteem? Is it your practical self that loses time and mental energy? What message does this part of you have for the rest of you?

_____

_____

_____

ACCEPTING OTHERS

A frequent challenge to accepting someone's secure attachment style is that it may be different from your own. In this way, it may feel unfamiliar or foreign. Most of us recognize love and care in the ways that we have seen and experienced. If someone cares for us in a different way, even if it *should* feel good, we may have a difficult time processing it as love or care.

For example, Tasha and Lyla had been together for six years and were deciding whether to get married. Tasha was securely attached, while Lyla had more of an insecure attachment with anxious behaviors. The following is an example of how secure attachment can seem perplexing to someone with an insecure attachment style:

> *"How can you be so sure we're right for each other?" Lyla asked.*
>
> *"I don't know what will happen in the future, but I think it will work. I know you'll work hard at the relationship, and I will, too," reasoned Tasha.*
>
> *"But sometimes I think I would be happier with someone who wants to live in the city and see the world. I fantasize about that."*
>
> *"Well, how important is that to you? I can go with you on some of your travels, and we can find a compromise on where we live."*
>
> *"I know, you've said that before." Lyla paused and thought for a few seconds, then her anxiety took a turn for the worse. "But how can you be so certain? What if I would just be happier with someone else?"*

There was no one else at present, but one trait of being insecurely attached is that it is difficult to make decisions and feel settled with them.

Tasha couldn't know the future, but she knew Lyla pretty well. She knew that Lyla had a tendency to balk at decisions and commitments, even when she would end up pretty happy with her decision. She had seen Lyla go through the same anxiety when it came to finding an apartment and choosing a grad school.

Tasha's confident reasoning wasn't always soothing to Lyla, though. Sometimes Lyla found it at best, wishful, and at worst, foolish. Her past experiences with close relationships taught her that good feelings with people don't last, and she came to expect relationships to change every few years. Tasha's comfort and expectation that their relationship would last was unfamiliar. It took Lyla a while before she could accept that their differences in attachment style were the reason for their different stances and that this was okay.

Relationship Strengths

What are your strengths and your partner's? As you interact with someone who has a secure attachment style, it can be helpful to remind yourself of your relationship strengths. Think about what you each contribute to the relationship and gifts that you share with one another. If you're not working on a romantic relationship right now, think in terms of whichever significant relationship you have in mind, whether that's a parent, sibling, best friend, or someone else.

Now that you've picked a specific relationship, go down the column for "Me" and place a check mark by each trait that is a strength you contribute to the relationship. Then go down the column for "My relationship partner" and do the same for the strengths they bring.

Me	My relationship partner	Strengths
		Honesty
		Fairness
		Willingness to put in hard work/effort
		Empathy
		Willingness to be open
		Trustworthiness
		Being a source of inspiration
		Commitment
		Collaboration
		Acceptance of faults
		Providing support
		Perseverance through rough times
		Dependability
		Consistency
		Ability to challenge the other in positive ways
		Playfulness
		Humor
		Readiness to express gratitude and appreciation
		Willingness to sacrifice
		Other:
		Other:

The ways in which you each contribute to the relationship may be the same or very different. If they're different, try to acknowledge that some of the ways in which your partner shares those skills and talents may feel unfamiliar at times. If so, try to be open to the new feeling of receiving them in this way, little by little.

Healthy Communication

Having close and meaningful relationships is generally regarded as one of the few variables that can predict happiness in life. These relationships make it possible for people to really share who they are with one another, be seen, and feel supported. Poor communication is often cited as one of the challenges to being happy in relationships.

A healthy approach to communication in close relationships takes into account that verbal communication is not, and never will be, perfect. People misspeak or misunderstand one another all the time, despite trying not to. We can only do our best, put our best intentions forward, and practice forgiveness when misunderstandings happen.

One of the central tenets of almost every healthy communication guide is to focus the speaker on sharing something about *themself* rather than the other person. Many communication experts encourage people to use "I statements," meaning statements that begin with the word *I* rather than *you*. Instead of saying, "You don't care about my feelings," you could say, "I don't feel met or cared for." The rule of using "I statements" can be a useful heuristic, but it also causes confusion because many statements beginning with *I* don't actually share something meaningful about the speaker, like "I think you are a jerk."

Is It a Meaningful "I Statement"?

The purpose of an "I statement" is to create an opportunity for more under-standing and connection by contributing something that you are the expert on: yourself. The more self-revealing an "I statement," the more meaningful it can be for communicating interpersonally with those you want to be close with. Here is an example of an "I statement" that, while simple, reveals some-thing about the speaker:

I went to the meeting early, because I don't like being late.

Here is an example of a statement beginning with *I* that does not accomplish the same sharing:

I thought the meeting started earlier than it did.

While this statement expresses a thought that the speaker had, it doesn't particularly reveal anything of substance about who the speaker is or their internal experience. We learn some context about the start of the meeting but not much else.

This exercise will help you practice detecting how self-revealing an "I statement" is. Read the following statements. If you think the statement reveals something meaningful about the speaker, circle *Yes*. If you believe it does not, circle *No*.

1. I am afraid of the dark.   Yes/No

2. I made you late.   Yes/No

3. I feel you've been disrespectful.   Yes/No

4. I need you to stop giving me directions.   Yes/No

5. I want us to work faster on the project.   Yes/No

6. I feel undesired.   Yes/No

7. I would feel grateful if you sat and talked with me.   Yes/No

8. I am relieved you got home safely.   Yes/No

9. I will never eat at that restaurant again.   Yes/No

Answer key with explanations:

1. Yes.

   I am afraid of the dark. This reveals an experience that the speaker understands about themself.

2. No.

   I made you late. While it might be appropriate to be accountable, this is not a revealing statement. The speaker is attributing fault to themself without any meaningful information about their own inner experience. A more revealing statement would be, "I feel regretful that I took longer than promised to get ready."

3. No.

   I feel you've been disrespectful. This statement expresses an evaluation but doesn't reveal anything about the speaker. Try instead, "I am not willing to tolerate the tone of voice you're using with me."

4. No.

   I need you to stop giving me directions. This statement sounds more like a demand and reveals nothing directly about the speaker. Try instead, "I'm too distracted to make use of your directions right now."

5. Yes.

   I want us to work faster on the project. This statement *does* reveal a want that the speaker has, but it could be stronger. Try instead, "I am excited about the idea of speeding up our workflow so we can all finish and leave early."

6. Yes.

   I feel undesired. This is a statement that clearly reveals an internal experience that only the speaker could know for sure. It's a great start.

7. Yes.

   I would feel grateful if you sat and talked with me. This statement clearly reveals a prediction about an internal experience.

8. Yes.

    I am relieved you got home safely. Again, this statement tells something about the internal experience of the speaker.

9. No.

    I will never eat at that restaurant again. This statement may be accurate when it comes to predicting future behavior, but it isn't particularly informative about what the speaker experienced at the restaurant. Try instead, "The food poisoning I had shook my confidence in eating there again." This statement does not begin with *I*, but it does reveal a lot more about what the speaker experienced. Fulfilling the spirit of an "I statement" does not always necessitate beginning the sentence with *I*.

Strengthening Your Bonds

When our close relationships are supportive and nourishing, we have a buffer from stress and room to grow and go further toward our goals. So far, we've looked at how developing trust, accepting ourselves and others as best we can, and communicating personally and clearly are key ingredients for supporting close relationships. To foster an even greater sense of positive connection and support in a relationship, I'd like to take a step further and talk about something that might get in the way of deepening relationship connections.

As children, most of us were taught the Golden Rule: Treat others as you would like to be treated. In general, this still applies. We generally want to treat others and be treated with kindness, accountability, and honesty.

However, in close relationships and love relationships, we also have the privilege of learning the very specific quirks and preferences of those we care about. We see them "up close and personal," because we've spent time with them and paid attention. We know what puts a smile on their face and what makes their day, and these things might be the same as or different from what makes us smile or makes our day.

Our most important relationships are special, because we can know people so well that there is an opportunity to tailor positive experiences that were meant for them.

Make Someone's Day

To create a culture of support and nourishment in your relationships, actively do things that will make someone's day. Putting in a bit of effort to create positive connection in your relationships will create warm feelings for both of you. So go ahead and fill out the following grid and commit to doing each of these things in the next week!

Someone in your life	Something I can do this week to make their day
Example: My brother	Example: Send a text that tells him how proud I am of him for finishing his degree.

Chapter Recap

- Secure attachment describes a style of bonding that is free from the stress of being close or depending on others.

- The body's resources are not focused on managing stress and threat, and thus can be used to solve problems in a relationship.

- Both secure and insecure approaches to a relationship can net an outcome or action that is similar on the surface. It takes digging into motivations, thoughts, and feelings in order to see the differences between the two.

The skills you can learn by working through this chapter include . . .

- How to differentiate between secure attachment behavior and behavior that is pseudosecure

- How to identify an "I statement" that contains meaningful self-revelation about the speaker

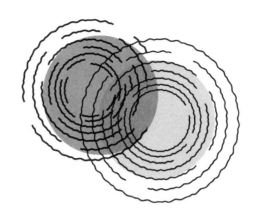

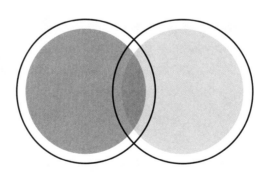

CHAPTER FIVE

Attachment Style Interactions

This chapter provides discussion and examples of specific combinations of attachment styles in relationships. Any combination of styles can create a relationship in which partners are strong and secure with one another, but each permutation also faces unique challenges.

It's important to remember that different relationships may bring out different aspects of your attachment style. Each relationship has its own signature that's made up of everything each partner brings, as well as the partners' shared history. Each person brings gifts and talents, and each also brings vulnerabilities and deficits.

Insecure attachment patterns show up in times of stress, such as when there's conflict, during big transitions and decision points in a relationship, when something outside the relationship is stressful for one or both partners, or in other difficult moments. Attachment styles often determine how people use the relationship with respect to that stressor. If they tend toward attachment anxiety, they may look for a lot of support and validation from their partner. If they tend toward attachment avoidance, they may prefer to keep their head down until the storm passes. If they are secure, they might go to some length to ensure that they both make it out of the stressful scenario together, closer, and safe.

For the most part, people can't help what kind of attachment reaction is natural to them. But if we let our insecure attachment patterns play out unchecked, we may be left wondering why the same relational problems keep cycling over and over. Eventually, we might want to put some conscious attention and effort into learning about our own and our partner's patterns.

What You'll Learn in This Chapter

In this chapter you will read about telltale signs of the six major attachment style interactions: anxious-anxious, avoidant-avoidant, anxious-avoidant, secure-anxious, secure-avoidant, and secure-secure. This information will help you develop your awareness of how your attachment style plays out in relationships and learn to identify the specific strengths and pitfalls that are common in each interaction. Through descriptions and examples of couples in each attachment style pairing, you'll see examples of how each can form a secure relationship and also examples of pitfalls that cause a pairing to be less secure.

This section also includes exercises for you and a partner that are geared toward developing secure connections, using play and rituals that inspire closeness. Although each attachment pairing will have a recommended exercise that addresses some of the specific pitfalls and strengths of the attachment style interaction, the exercises aren't relevant just to romantic partnerships. To find a partner for the exercise, simply share it with someone close to you, let the person know why you would like to try it with them, and ask if they would like to work on it with you.

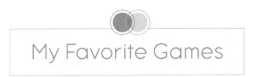

My Favorite Games

You'd do well to approach this chapter with an open, playful frame of mind. Do you remember the excitement and imagination of playing games when you were a child? Your brain was at its best in learning and figuring out small puzzles with others who were doing the same. Playfulness is beneficial for adults, as well, improving our ability to connect, think, be creative, and experience positive emotions.

To refresh your memory of what it was like to play, list three to five of your favorite games that you remember playing, as either a child or an adult:

_____

_____

_____

_____

_____

As you move through this chapter, try to keep the same playful attitude you felt when you played those games!

The Anxious-Anxious Interaction

Two people on the anxious end of the spectrum are likely to be passionate relationship partners who both worry about being abandoned when things get stressful. Anxious-anxious pairings tend to be passionate, because there is a tendency for the partners to hold little back—they are open and giving, occasionally to a fault.

The worst-case scenario for these couples, and the conflict that will probably cause the most distress, is when both partners feel abandoned by the other. Triggers for this feeling of abandonment will vary from person to person, but with partners who are anxiously attached, it usually finds a way to show itself in big or small ways. This is the case for Beth and Cece.

Beth and Cece are in their late 30s and have been best friends for over a decade. Both friends have an anxious attachment style. They both are lawyers and love a good argument. Over the years, there have been some minor incidents in their friendship that have highlighted their attachment insecurity, such as when Beth felt abandoned when Cece didn't invite her to a music festival or when Cece felt hurt that Beth wasn't available to give her advice about a case. They always worked these conflicts out and felt good about their friendship after doing so.

The first time their relationship security was tested was when Cece got married and had a child. Suddenly, Cece might take a week to return Beth's call, whereas before, she always called back the same day. Due to her new family obligations, Cece was just less available. Beth also found herself feeling intensely jealous of the new friendships Cece made with other parents in her neighborhood.

While Cece was glad to be starting her family, she was overwhelmed with the obligations and responsibilities of marriage and motherhood. She felt envious of Beth's freedom and felt the absence of their closeness as an abandonment. She wanted Beth to show more interest in her family and resented Beth for making what she felt was too little effort to keep up their friendship.

For months, they complained to one another about what they perceived as the other's slights, and they both ended up feeling defensive for being "accused" by the other. Cece felt blamed for getting married and starting a family. Beth was resentful that Cece seemed to think it was Beth's job to make an extra effort to maintain their friendship now that Cece had a kid. Both felt abandoned by the other.

Eventually, though, they recognized they were having the same feelings—that they both missed each other and were both uncertain about how to sustain a friendship given the changes in their lives. Once they put a pause on blaming each other for the tensions they were having, they saw how invested they both were in the friendship. Fighting with each other was just a misguided way of showing it.

Couples and other relationship partners with an anxious-anxious dynamic are prone to lengthy processing sessions filled with blaming statements. Their intentions are rarely malicious. Instead, they both want badly to find satisfying solutions and are willing to work hard to do so. But even with all this hard work, the presence of insecurity and anxiety creates panic and can hijack good intentions. Feeling chronically insecure makes it all too easy to make fear-based interpretations of your loved one's behavior, just as Beth and Cece did when they felt abandoned. The typical result for these relationships is that the partners find themselves recycling the same fight over and over, despite their best efforts to break out of the rut.

If both people can be aware of this sensitivity being triggered, use healthy communication, and respond in an understanding way, it can turn a panic situation into an opportunity for appreciation of how well they know each other and how much they value their connection. Anxiously attached people also have a visceral understanding of how painful it is to feel abandoned, so there is the potential for deep empathy and connection.

"No, No, Yes" Game

Healthy boundaries are a cornerstone of secure relationships. In order to have healthy boundaries, it is necessary to learn how *yes* looks and feels, and how *no* looks and feels, for yourself and for your partner. For anxious people, saying no can be difficult or scary. In this game, you will pay close attention to yourself and your partner as you each take turns saying no to one another for several rounds before you feel comfortable saying yes.

For the partner who is making the request and hearing *no* repeatedly, it is also an opportunity to make requests based on collaboration, using the feedback loop to refine your approach, and to keep trying new and different tactics. This is a great game for sharpening your nonverbal communication skills and more effectively using body language, voice tone and inflection, and eye contact—and remember to keep your playful attitude!

1. Sit comfortably across from one another at a close enough distance that you can easily make eye contact and read each other's expressions. Decide who will be Partner A and who will be Partner B.

2. Partner A: Your job is to make a request by repeating one word, "Please," in different ways, until Partner B says yes. You cannot use any other words, but you can say it with different emotions, attitudes, and tones. You can also use body language and eye contact to communicate different approaches. If it is helpful, you can think of a specific request for what the "Please" represents, but don't share this with your partner. Keep trying different approaches until your partner says yes.

3. Partner B: Your job is to say no to the first attempt and keep saying no until you feel a genuine shift to *yes*. If it is helpful, you can think of a specific request that your partner is making, but don't share it with your partner.

Questions for discussion:

- How did you feel when you said no?
- When was it easiest to say no?
- What did it feel like in your body when you noticed a shift to *yes*?
- What did you see in your partner that made you want to say yes?
- If you didn't say yes in one of the rounds, then what could your partner have done to help you get to a genuine *yes*?

Notes:

_____

_____

_____

_____

_____

The Avoidant-Avoidant Interaction Style

The early years of an avoidant-avoidant pairing often feel easy. "Conflict? What conflict? We get along so well." These folks enter into an unspoken pact: "I won't rock the boat if you won't."

Long before he was in the White House, Donald Trump described his approach to marriage shortly after marrying his third wife, Melania. "We just have this natural relationship. . . . I don't want to go home and have to work at a relationship. A relationship where you have to work at it doesn't work." Melania echoed this approach. "He's working all the time. . . . I don't want to change him; I don't want to say, 'Come home and be with me.' I don't want to change him. I want to give him space. I think that's important in the relationship." Their descriptions of their marriage echo the early stages of an avoidant-avoidant relationship. In the early stage, it can seem to work very well, because the pair stay out of each other's way when it comes to anything that could cause upset. They happily enjoy the aspects of the relationship that are ideal and easy, and ignore the rest.

Over time, this model of relationship can break down when one or both people's needs and wants evolve, and they desire something from the relationship that is a challenge for the other to provide. This unmet need becomes unbearable when one partner breaks that unspoken pact and starts to complain. When this happens, it can look more like an anxious-avoidant dynamic. The complaints may be indirect at first, but if things don't improve, eventually the frustration and hostility will increase until it's clear that the relationship will be in trouble if they don't do something different.

Zion and Venessa married 12 years ago. They met out dancing one night and fell in love right away. Zion's friends describe him as a fun, dynamic individual, and Venessa's friends characterize her as very giving, responsible, and talented. They always have fun together, except when they have to talk about anything serious or conflictual. That's when the jokes dry up and their body language stiffens. Both are sensitive to one another's distress and so try not to "burden" the other with relationship problems.

They have their ways of avoiding. Together, they use humor and diversion. Venessa travels for work and probably takes more travel assignments than she needs to. Zion denies his own feelings of frustration, hurt, and anger in the name of "taking care of Venessa." This became stressful for him, and eventually he developed mysterious digestion problems. After several years of the relationship proceeding in this way, he could no longer hold it in. He began to voice his dissatisfaction, which surprised them both. Venessa found that when Zion expressed his dissatisfaction or anger, it triggered a backlog of her own anger at events that had never been resolved between the two of them. And very quickly, the conflicts would escalate.

Venessa and Zion found themselves in this situation because they had gotten so good at staying out of each other's way. Once Pandora's box was open, it could never be closed again. In order for them both to feel good about the relationship again, they had to untrain themselves from avoiding conflict and learn the skills to deal with each of the issues that were backlogged. They also had to teach themselves how to address problems as they arose so they wouldn't end up back in the same place a few years down the road.

Eventually, the couple made progress. They enjoyed their relationship again after a period of learning to consciously check in with one another, rather than keeping a superficial peace between them. Avoidance of conflict is not harmony. The couple had to learn to be less wary of conflict and use new tools to deal with their differences in a way that didn't feel so scary.

Avoidant-avoidant pairings veer toward insecurity, because the more that's avoided, the more precarious it is to maintain real security in a relationship. The strategy of avoidance allows you to kick the can down the road, but eventually, somebody has to account for the changing needs and wants, or risk losing the relationship. In later stages, relationships that stay avoidant feel too much like the emotional equivalent of walking in a field of land mines, and the time and effort that are required to navigate around them becomes so great that it overshadows enjoyment of one another.

Feelings Check-in

Relationships can fall into a rut and people can drift apart when there is a lack of conscious effort to be revealing and open about personal needs. One simple way to practice deepening the relationship is by making the effort to check in on a regular basis using *feeling words* rather than talking about superficial events or just telling each other you're fine. Identifying more precise feelings may seem like a minor thing, but it can make a huge difference in strengthening intimacy in relationships. This exercise can be done either with a partner or on your own. Use the "feeling" words in this chart to carry out the exercise that follows.

Feelings Inventory

Negative high arousal	Disconnection	Negative low arousal
Afraid	Aloof	Bored
Aggressive	Defensive	Depressed
Annoyed	Disappointed	Despairing
Anxious	Distant	Discouraged
Bitter	Distracted	Disheartened
Confused	Distrustful	Gloomy
Doubtful	Humiliated	Heavyhearted
Enraged	Indifferent	Hopeless
Frazzled	Jealous	Insignificant
Frightened	Protective	Melancholy
Helpless	Resentful	Numb
Indecisive	Wary	Sad
Indignant	Withdrawn	Skeptical
Infuriated		Unhappy
Irritated		Uninterested
Nervous		
Overwhelmed		
Panicked		
Provoked		
Upset		
Worried		

Positive low arousal	Connection	Positive high arousal
Calm	Accepted	Amazed
Centered	Affectionate	Astonished
Comfortable	Appreciative	Creative
Content	Curious	Eager
Peaceful	Friendly	Empowered
Pleased	Grateful	Energetic
Quiet	Loving	Enlivened
Relaxed	Openhearted	Enthusiastic
Safe	Playful	Excited
Satisfied	Respected	Hopeful
Serene	Secure	Joyful
	Sympathetic	Passionate
	Touched	Proud
	Trusting	Surprised
	Valued	

1. Make a commitment with a partner or to yourself that for the next week, you will do a daily feelings check-in. This can be very simple or more elaborate, with some explanation for why you are feeling that way. Try to challenge yourself to be more descriptive than you might normally. You must use a feeling word and cannot just say you feel okay, fine, or anything that general. You may use the Feelings Inventory on page 122 to help you identify specific feeling words. Log them into the calendar on the next page for later discussion.

2. Agree on when and how this check-in will work best for both of you. It could be in person, over the phone, or by text message. It can be as simple as, "Let's check in. What are you feeling today?" Also, discuss whether you want your partner to respond with encouragement, appreciation, nothing at all, or something else. If doing the exercise on your own, write your responses down in a notebook.

3. After the week is over, debrief with the discussion questions following the Feelings Inventory.

Calendar of Feelings Check-ins

Day	My feeling	Partner's feeling
Monday		
Tuesday		
Wednesday		
Thursday		
Friday		
Saturday		
Sunday		

Discussion questions:

- How different was this experience from how you normally share your feelings with people?
- What did you learn about yourself?
- What did you learn about your partner?
- How likely are you to continue to check in using feeling words?

Notes:

_____

_____

_____

The Anxious-Avoidant Interaction

In attachment theory, this pairing—one anxious person and one avoidant person—is often called the *distancer-pursuer* dynamic. You both have a sixth sense for threats, but your instincts move you in opposite directions. Instead of intuitively understanding the other's behavior, you are both more likely to be confused and hurt by it, further driving your original insecurities. The misunderstanding can then become more extreme, with one partner entreating and the other retreating.

Abel and Xavier are university professors in their early 50s who have partnered professionally for more than a decade on their research. They both have wives, but even their wives acknowledge that in many ways, their husbands' research and relationship with one another take precedence over their marriages.

Abel has a more avoidant attachment style, while Xavier's style is more anxious. Their conflicts sometimes used to go further than just robust intellectual debate. They depend on one another for validation, stimulation, companionship, and mutual respect. These are things they both value very much.

The friends care for one another deeply, but their relationship had complications. They competed with one another academically, which sometimes put them at odds. Abel's more affable personality meant that he often got more public attention for their joint publications, which sometimes left Xavier feeling as if he'd been taken advantage of or even rejected.

Because of Xavier's anxious attachment, he found himself in panic about being abandoned by Abel and losing the connection he so valued. He interpreted Abel's publicity as attention seeking and felt left out. Being undervalued and left out was something Xavier had felt when younger, so he was very sensitive to that dynamic as an adult. Xavier began to protest in big and small ways. He accused Abel of being selfish and threatened to stop working with him.

But seeking attention never was Abel's aim; he was just polite and said yes to those who inquired about the research, because he didn't like saying no and wanted to build a positive reputation. Having an insecure avoidant style, Abel also made some predictable errors and misinterpretations about anxious Xavier and what was really upsetting him. When Xavier confronted Abel about leaving him seemingly uncredited for his contributions to their work, or when he generally seemed gloomy, Abel interpreted this as Xavier criticizing his character. This left him feeling that he couldn't do anything right, something Abel was sensitive about. Xavier's protests felt like attacks and left Abel feeling cornered. He tried to smooth things over again and again but would eventually get fed up and attack back.

Things didn't get better for Xavier and Abel until they finally learned to understand and take seriously their own and each other's emotional hurt. Abel learned to listen and respond more thoughtfully to Xavier, and Xavier learned to express his grievances in a way that was less threatening to Abel. They worked to ensure that their shared projects were represented as a joint effort and tried to promote their work together whenever possible. The men were initially reluctant to change their ways, but when it came down to it, their friendship was worth protecting, even if it meant risking change.

Play as Animals

Couples who find themselves in an anxious-avoidant dynamic often get stuck in their patterns, as each becomes more rigid in their particular response to feeling attachment stress and threat. According to neuroscientist Stephen Porges, play is the antidote to threat. In relationships where partners have a strong baseline of insecurity, it helps to have as many tools to promote safety and playfulness as possible. This game is one of those tools, and it's likely to elicit movement, laughs, and joy.

1. Recall the last two or three disagreements the two of you had, and come to an agreement on which one you will re-create for this game.
2. Each partner picks an animal. It could be your favorite animal or another. You'll use your imagination to mimic the movements and sounds your animal makes.
3. Re-create what the disagreement was about using only movements and sounds your animal makes. You can bark, meow, roar, slither, pounce, or scurry. No human language!
4. Set the timer for 10 minutes and stop when time is up or when there is a resolution to the fight.
5. When time is up, discuss what it was like with one another, using the guiding questions below.

Questions to discuss:
• How did you experience yourself differently in animal form?
• How did you experience your partner differently in animal form?
• What surprised you about doing the exercise?

Notes:

The Secure-Anxious Interaction

Relationships that feature secure-anxious interactions can go in either a more secure or a more anxious direction, depending on how the participants handle conflict and sometimes also depending on who is the more dominant person in the relationship. The more anxious person tends to call attention to themself because they often feel emotions with more urgency and is apt to act and speak more impulsively. Interactions work better when the anxious partner learns to self-soothe and be more self-reflective or when the more secure partner can learn to help the anxious partner when necessary. The following is an example of a secure-anxious couple and how they get into—and out of—the kind of trouble this partnership can bring.

Terrence is primarily securely attached. Two years ago, he married Bess, who has strong anxious tendencies. Recently, a conflict escalated between Bess and Terrence's sister, resulting in Bess being disinvited from her baby shower. This caused tension within Terrence's family, and Bess has been distraught ever since. Bess was bullied as a child by her sisters, which reinforced her fear of rejection in close relationships as well as her anxious response to these fears as they played out in her adult relationships. Now, real or imagined, this conflict involved her extended family, and it was devastating.

Terrence had been navigating through this difficult situation as he had always done with Bess whenever she felt anxious. Typical of a secure type, he was quick to disarm her using jokes, laughter, and a very warm, sincere support that in the past had always proved effective at reassuring her. But with this situation, it wasn't working. Even though Terrence wasn't taking any particular side in the conflict, and wasn't particularly close to his sister, Bess could see only her own magnified pain and found it difficult to disassociate Terrence or his parents from his sister's actions. This is somewhat typical of insecure anxious folks; when in a reactive pattern, they project their anxiety and distress on everything they see.

Bess turned to Terrence, hoping he could somehow offset his sister's rejection by affirming his allegiance to her. But Terrence felt torn between his wife and his family, and was ineffective at giving Bess what she needed.

They came to an impasse when Bess asked Terrence to cut ties with his sister, which he refused to do. Characteristic of secure attachment, he just plainly told her this, rather than escalate a fight about it (the anxious response) or sidestep the request (an avoidant response).

Through counseling, they learned to build a framework for protecting their bond that also allowed them to have respect for individual family relationships. Terrence learned to validate Bess's feelings and address her fears more specifically. As Bess worked to resolve her individual trauma of being bullied, she was better able to hold the boundary of her emotions and felt less threatened and more confident in her bond with Terrence.

Bess and Terrence's relationship had already benefited from his securely attached sensibilities, as his calm and caring demeanor had previously helped her feel safe despite her anxious tendencies. Where they needed help was when family relationships complicated how effective he was at helping Bess feel prioritized and protected. Terrence could not in good conscience do what Bess wanted, as cutting off his sister was too high a price to pay. In the end, they were able to resolve the issue to both their satisfaction by being open to external support and facilitation.

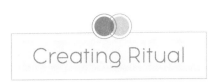

Creating Ritual

Rituals are actions and practices that symbolize something important. Having rituals in your relationships is a great way to regularly engage in reminders of your shared values. This exercise will help you create a very special ritual for you and your loved one that will help both partners feel safe and secure.

1. Pick one of the following relationship values that you both agree is important to your vision for your relationship, or each choose your own:

   ☐ Kindness

   ☐ Give-and-take

   ☐ Appreciation and gratitude

   ☐ Affection

   ☐ Openness

   ☐ Playfulness

   ☐ Commitment

   ☐ Joy

2. Think of a simple activity or action you can do together that symbolizes this value in some small way. It can be a very simple act, but in the creation of shared meaning, it becomes a special ritual. Here is an example of a ritual for each value above that centers around tea:

   Kindness: *Take turns each night making tea for one another.*

   Give-and-take: *Make each other's tea in the morning.*

   Appreciation and gratitude: *Toast one another before drinking your tea.*

   Affection: *Cuddle on the couch together while drinking tea.*

   Openness: *Talk about your day together over tea.*

   Playfulness: *Take turns surprising each other with a new flavor of tea.*

   Commitment: *Share the same flavor of tea every night.*

Joy: Have a tea party once a week with dancing and music.

3. Agree on how often you will do the ritual together and a time to begin. If it makes sense, agree to have something you can do each day that you see each other.

Record your unique ritual and what it means here:

_____

_____

_____

The Secure-Avoidant Interaction

The secure-avoidant relationship can just as easily default to avoidance as it can to more secure traits. If the secure partner does not take the lead to really learn the avoidant partner's pattern, they might get surprised down the road.

Joyce and Julio are a married couple in their 30s. After eight years together, Joyce discovered that Julio had developed a relationship with another woman, sending and receiving messages that were emotionally intense and sexually explicit. Julio ended it when Joyce found out, but they came to therapy to see if they could heal and repair their trust. This was a case of infidelity where their attachment styles were at the forefront of why the affair had happened. Joyce's attachment style was primarily secure, while Julio's was primarily avoidant.

Julio idealized Joyce and constantly worried that he wasn't good enough for her. Fearful of losing her, he struggled when bringing up topics like finances or anything that might upset her. He covered up or avoided potential sources of conflict because he feared she would leave him. Without the freedom to speak his mind, he felt constrained by the marriage. The outside relationship helped him feel that he had an insurance policy if Joyce ended up leaving him, as part of him always suspected she would.

Joyce acknowledged that she had grown complacent in the upkeep of their marriage. Since Julio was all too happy to say that things were fine, it was easy for her to believe it. At one point, when she harbored suspicions about his cheating and asked him, he denied it. She backed off after that, despite her gut telling her otherwise. Part of her also wanted to believe there was nothing more to know.

Joyce's secure attachment style showed in her evenhanded reaction to Julio's cheating. She felt betrayed and shocked, and showed it, but was measured in her response and constantly showed her intention to gather more information, get help, and not jump to conclusions about what had happened or what it meant about their relationship.

Their marriage became stronger when Joyce started asking more questions about what Julio was up to when it came to finances, other relationships, and his true feelings about their life together. Because Joyce tended to be so measured and unthreatening, this helped him come out of his shell and take risks toward having a more open and honest relationship. Over time, Julio gained more confidence that Joyce accepted him despite his flaws.

Intimate Discussions

Meaningful relationships are built on a foundation of knowledge about one another that others don't know or haven't taken the time to learn. Getting to know someone is a process based on curiosity, interaction, and feedback. This process takes the courage to *share* as much as it takes a willingness to understand and see the other person. This exercise will give you both an opportunity to practice having conversations that invite greater intimacy.

1. Find a comfortable place to sit across from your partner, and choose who will go first.
2. During each person's "turn," they will state the question provided, then follow with an attempt to guess how the partner would answer the question. The "sentence stems" below can help you answer.
3. After each attempt at guessing the other's response, ask your partner, "Is that close?" and allow them to make corrections or confirmations as needed. During this time, you will listen to your partner without interrupting. When they are done, thank your partner for clarifying, then move to the next question.
4. When you have answered all four questions, switch roles.

Questions and sentence stems:

- What is most important to you? I think what is most important to you is . . .
- What don't you want me to know about you? I think you don't want me to know . . .
- Do you trust me with your life? I think you do/don't trust me with your life because . . .
- What do you dislike most about yourself? I think you might dislike . . .

Please write down anything you noticed about the exercise or that surprised you:

_____

_____

_____

_____

_____

The Secure-Secure Interaction

Unsurprisingly, secure-secure pairings are pleasant to be involved in and pleasant to be around. These couples seem fair with one another and never throw the other under the bus to protect themselves. They flow easily between their individual interests and the common goals they share. These couples are also very good at catching misunderstandings when they communicate and at clearing things up quickly, rather than letting bad feelings fester.

It's natural to assume that these couples have it easy and have totally solid relationships. But there are also times when these relationships get tested, just as does any other. Let's consider a couple who embody this combination so we can see examples of typical strengths and challenges.

Holly and Leroy both come from a secure attachment background. They have been together over 12 years; they knew one another in high school and started dating in college. At their best, they enjoy a relationship that feels, and is, rock solid. They have everyday quibbles, of course, but they're very good at taking time to listen to one another and staying open to changing their views. They try to give one another the benefit of the doubt and generally steer clear of holding grudges. Since both have a relatively secure style of relating, this has always been somewhat natural for them.

Because they met early in their lives, they've had a long history of supporting each other, particularly in their careers. Holly is a management consultant and Leroy recently decided to make a career change from marketing to education, something he only recently recognized as a passion. Leroy has begun a master's program in education and, for the first time in his life, feels invigorated with purpose and surrounded by intellectually stimulating conversations.

As Leroy has spent more time with his fellow students, studying, working, and observing in classrooms, he's found that he has more and more in common with them. He has developed deep friendships with his classmates based on intellectual curiosity, love of cultural events, and shared values. He's realized that though he and Holly love each other, she just doesn't share many of these interests with him. At first, he tried to involve her in his newfound passions, but they never really appealed to her. This was okay, but it created a widening rift between the two. Holly saw this happening but didn't know what to do about it. She had also grown rather complacent in the comfort of their dynamic and did not expect that Leroy could or would do anything that would actively threaten the relationship.

As you can tell, transitions in life can lead to some pretty major challenges to relationship security. People change, and if there isn't enough attention given to finding ways to prioritize the relationship and shepherd it through the changes, transitions can pose a threat or disruption.

Leroy and Holly already have good practice with some of the tools needed to get through this disruption in their relationship security. Because they are both securely attached, they are able to take turns listening to one another and really considering the other's perspective.

However, they will need to decide whether prioritizing their relationship continues to make sense, given the major shifts and growth Leroy is experiencing. If they both conclude that the relationship is valuable enough to continue, they will have to break out of the complacency and comfort they have developed together in order to pay attention to their growing and changing needs, and respond with their best collaborative, creative efforts.

If they decide to go their separate ways, their breakup will likely be informed by their securely attached ways. The breakup will be well considered and mutual, and they'll give each other enough closure to move on in a healthy way.

Securely attached partners, whether in commitment or when separating, consider each other's needs and try to be fair. Despite their secure attachment, these partners sometimes end or make major changes to their relationships for the same reasons as in all relationships, when they grow apart or are at the intersection of major life transitions.

Quiet Love

Prolonged eye contact is a very effective way of bringing two people into close intimacy and promoting feelings of warmth and safety. When two people first make eye contact, no matter how well they know each other, there can be a sense of alertness—unfamiliarity, even. But when you each continue with long, easy breaths, relaxing into the eye gaze, you enter into a state of "quiet love" associated with the activation of oxytocin and other bonding hormones.

1. Sit down comfortably, facing your partner. Set the timer for at least 5 minutes and as many as 30.
2. Gaze into your partner's eyes. You can blink normally, but try not to look away. If you notice your gaze wandering off, simply bring it back to meet your partner's eyes.
3. Share with your partner what you experienced. Consider the following prompts:

   - Did anything surprise you?
   - What was difficult about the exercise?
   - What was easy about the exercise?
   - How connected did you feel before the exercise? How connected during and after?

Notes:

_____

_____

_____

_____

_____

Chapter Recap

- There are six primary attachment style interactions: anxious-anxious, avoidant-avoidant, anxious-avoidant, secure-anxious, secure-avoidant, and secure-secure.

- Each interaction has certain predictable characteristics, relationship challenges, and strengths.

- Regardless of attachment styles, relationship security relies on ongoing attention to each other, efforts to under-stand one another, and having a shared vision you can come back to time and time again.

The skills you can learn by working through this chapter include . . .

- How to use ritual, play, discussion, and nonverbal commu-nication to strengthen your relationship and bring about greater closeness.

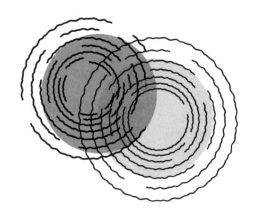

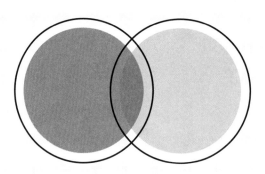

CHAPTER SIX

Building a Secure Future

The Long Haul

Building healthy relationships is an ongoing, lifelong process. Even people who tend toward the secure attachment style will have ups and downs, and will encounter new relationship dynamics that test their strengths. The best thing any of us can do is stay in touch with those parts of ourselves that still struggle with anxious or avoidant attachment and keep using the resources we need to heal. Understanding and healing your attachment insecurity has the potential to positively affect *all* your relationships.

Modern science doesn't yet know everything about the brain, but there is wide agreement that this complex organ evolved in large part to enable us to have relationships and communicate with others. It's natural for us to seek the support of others from birth throughout the life span. It's what our brains were meant to do. But attachment insecurity and learned behavior patterns of anxiety and avoidance get in the way of safety and trust in these relationships.

The journey to healing attachment insecurity is complex and evolves over time. Romantic partnerships can bring up a lot of these issues and can be complicated most by attachment insecurity because of the degree of emotional dependence often found in these relationships.

Relationships have evolved to be extremely complex, with immense choice in how we engage with others whom we trust, commit our time to, and cultivate emotional safety and security with. Within this large arena of options, I invite you to remember your basic values when it comes to relationships of all kinds and to call upon skills and tools to put these values into practice.

Healing the Anxious Self

If you recognized aspects of yourself in the descriptions of anxious attachment in this book, then you know that what your brain and nervous system do under certain kinds of relationship stress is not the same as who you are in relationship. If the ways your body and brain respond don't work for you, you have the power to make changes to align better with your relationship values.

One of your first steps is to find some acceptance for the thoughts, feelings, and body sensations that make up your experience of relationships. Forgive the things you have done in the past that haven't worked or that have even created hurt. Show yourself compassion when it comes to where you are in your development.

Here are some relevant steps toward more secure relationships:

- Have patience with people, while staying connected to your needs and wants
- Know that when people can't meet your needs, it's not personal to you
- Identify what attachment repair looks like for you and others

Desiree was a client who showed tremendous movement from attachment anxiety toward security. Looking back at her history, Desiree could tell that anxious attachment had played a role in every romantic relationship she ever had. Usually, she would get quite serious in a relationship with the hope that it would be "the one." But when her partners let her down, her behavior would turn more chaotic and blaming, eventually driving them away.

She was tired of this cycle and wanted to learn how to find what worked for her in relationships. She began therapy, read as much as she could on these topics, and talked to respected people in her community. Little by little, she was able to apply the ideas to her own life. She decided that she wouldn't enter into a serious romantic relationship until she felt more confident in her relationship skills.

This freed Desiree up to focus more on her community and friendships, and she began to feel it was possible to have a full life outside romantic partnership. She worked on sharing her needs and wants with people without feeling too bad if someone couldn't meet them. Your healing path may or may not look like Desiree's, but however and with whomever you do your healing, you may encounter similar themes.

Healing the Avoidant Self

If you recognize avoidant attachment in yourself, and if it has had a negative effect on your relationships, the first thing to remember is that you're not to blame. These patterns were established long before you could make decisions, and without major formative experiences to correct early injuries, you continued to engage in your familiar pattern.

Here are some steps you can take to build more secure relationships:

- Get comfortable with having needs and wants
- Practice sharing more about yourself with the people you care about
- Learn ways of working out differences with others
- Learn to repair with another person when they feel injured by you

Ali was a client who enjoyed success in managing his avoidant attachment style. Ali was a welder in a steel factory, a physically strenuous environment where injuries and accidents were common. While handling a very sensitive piece of equipment, he forgot an important step and sustained a severe injury that required rushing to the emergency room. After 28 stitches and some reflection, Ali identified feeling hurt that none of his coworkers asked how he was doing.

Ali's coworkers weren't callous people. Actually, it was a very supportive and team-oriented work environment. The primary reason Ali had not received much sympathy was because he had unknowingly trained them to expect deflection if they expressed care for him. By now, they had learned that there was no point. With any injury in the shop, big or small, Ali would write it off as "no big deal."

After some time in therapy, Ali learned to recognize his specific needs, wants, and boundaries in his relationships. He found that when he relaxed more and shared himself with people, they opened up to him, too. He even got comfortable making requests at times.

Sharing your needs, vulnerabilities, and wants may not feel easy for you. You'll probably stumble or feel embarrassed. This is normal with *anything* unfamiliar. Feel some confidence that by committing to yourself and your relationship values, you'll create welcome changes.

Lasting Security

Lasting security in relationship comes from the ongoing work you put into getting to know yourself and the people you care about. This is work that, for many, pays off in spades. You know, because you can begin to enjoy connections with people and lean on them when you are hurt or feel alone.

As you learn about and accept the feelings and thoughts that inform your responses, you'll also get more comfortable navigating them and be able to make thoughtful choices based on the vision you have for your relationships. All this just takes some practice. For your hard work, I hope and believe you'll see that new and hopeful relationship experiences are possible.

Emotional safety and support produce lasting security, and now you are your own best consultant on what it's going to take to get it. Remember that getting things right in relationships involves experience and experimentation. You may find that you value deep and intimate connection with one person. Or you may find that three best friends fulfill your vision for lasting security. Our brains are wired for connection, but there is no rigid formula for what that looks like. I encourage you to find whatever works for you.

Envisioning Your Future

Take a moment to imagine a positive and connected vision of your future. These are the visions that will come into greater focus as you refine your relationship skills. Imagine what you really want to see a year from today, and consider the following questions:

A year from today, which relationships do you care most about and are most involved with?

_____

_____

_____

_____

_____

_____

As you build confidence in your ability to feel more secure, skillful, and collaborative in your relationships, what are you doing differently?

_____

_____

_____

_____

_____

_____

How do the people you love respond to your new behavior?

_____

_____

_____

_____

_____

_____

The Path Forward

Congratulations for the work you have put into improving your relationships! It takes courage to examine your own attitudes and behaviors with the intention of developing yourself. As you forge ahead in your relationships, remember that there is always room for mistakes and setbacks; it just makes the experience of growth richer. The resources, journaling, and values-based exercises in this book can be tools for you to return to whenever you need.

I've seen people make great strides toward relationship security. Every time I have the opportunity to witness their effort is humbling. Thank you for your work in this endeavor, and please know that your efforts don't stand alone. With more and more people committing to better relationships, for themselves and the people they love, we can help create a movement that changes society and how we understand and treat one another.

Blank Worksheets

You can download other worksheets at
CallistoMediaBooks.com/AttachmentTheory.

Tracing Your Anxious Attachment Pattern

Let's turn now to an exercise that will help you understand what your anxious attachment behavior is really about. You'll dig deep into an uncomfortable experience, but the goal is to help you understand how this attachment style works in your relationships.

1. Think of something that happened in a relationship that made you feel bad or uncomfortable. What happened to trigger this feeling?

The incident that triggered my bad or uncomfortable feeling:

_____

_____

2. Incidents hurt people for reasons that are personal to each individual. If we zoom in on your experience of the event you just noted, what was the worst part about it *to you*?

_____

_____

_____

The worst part about the incident for me:

_____

_____

Nice job for allowing yourself to be curious about your own feelings and experiences, and why they affect you uniquely! This understanding is an important part of being able to manage your feelings.

Here's a bonus exercise; while it's optional, it can be extremely helpful in understanding the pattern of this feeling across your life. Below is a timeline from birth to 20 years of age. The first couple of decades of our experiences can be very formative. If we didn't have help managing the difficult things we thought and felt during this time, they can affect how we view others and ourselves later in life.

Consider your first two decades of life. When was the first time you recall having the feeling or experience, or one similar to it? Put an X on that part of the timeline.

1	2	3	4	5	6	7	8	9	10	11	12	13	14	15	16	17	18	19	20

Age

Most incidents that evoke big feelings do so because those feelings have their origin in early life. Did you put an X somewhere on this timeline? If so, this is very normal. Now go forward on the timeline and put an X on the different ages when you remember having this same feeling. Try to put at least three X marks on the timeline and as many as you would like. Consider experiences you've had with people at home, school, work, church, and so on.

Put down your pen or pencil and take a deep breath. You are now viewing the legacy of this feeling or experience in your life. Take a look at the timeline and consider the following questions:

1. How does it look overall? Are there more *X* marks concentrated in one area, or are they spread out?
2. Did anything surprise you?
3. Are there certain kinds of relationships where you tend to experience this feeling more?
4. Has anyone or anything ever helped you go through this feeling with more ease?

Soothing Anxious Attachment

This exercise will help you identify your own way of approaching conflict with someone in your life who is anxiously attached. Think of someone in your life who can be rather abrasive and express their needs in a critical or pessimistic way. What is your natural response when they behave this way?

_____

_____

_____

How do they usually respond in return?

_____

_____

_____

With that pattern identified, think about what behaviors might be more helpful for you when responding to anxious attachment. Here are some suggestions to help your loved one in a moment of panic and anxiety. Put a check next to the ones that you already do or have tried.

☐ Reassurance. "I'm here." "I'm not going anywhere."

☐ Proximity and contact in a way that is appropriate for the relationship. If the person is your romantic partner, use loving touch and embrace. If not, step forward, make kind eye contact and smile, or if appropriate, hold their hand.

☐ Take the lead. Help manage the person's anxiety with clear and simple directives. People in a state of panic are more primed for understanding short phrases. "Stop." "Slow down." "Tell me something nice." "Give me a moment to think."

☐ Pace their expectations and anticipation. "Let's talk about that in a few minutes, when we're calm." "We'll talk about that after we finish this."

☐ Ask for specific feedback. "How did the way we talked work for you this time?"

Which of these would you like to try the next time you encounter anxious behavior? Write them below, making them specific to your relationship with the anxious individual:

_____

_____

_____

_____

Map Your Emotions

Emotions have both a mental and a physical component, and we can feel resistant to one or the other or both. Directing our attention to the specific bodily experiences that are connected to an emotion can help facilitate greater acceptance of that emotion. Since anger is such a powerful emotion, try this next exercise to see how it works for you.

Recall the last time you were angry with someone close to you. Can you feel just a little of what it was like? Where do you feel it in your body?

Imagine what size/shape/temperature/color/quality the feeling has.

When did it appear?

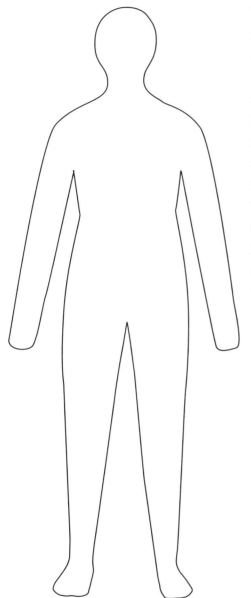

Using a pen or pencil, colored, if you wish, make a sketch of what you feel on the part of the body where you feel it.

Now, take a deep breath. Even imagining anger can bring the feeling into your body! Acknowledge that sometimes this feeling is in your body and sometimes it is not. Practice telling yourself that there's no need to fight it. When the feeling is there, try to accept its physical presence, and keep an open and even curious mind about what it is there for. Learning how to manage strong emotions in this way can be helpful when you are triggered.

Safety and Security Needs

Consent is only the first step. When it comes to attachment, there are two needs: safety and security. Safety is about relief from an experience of threat in the body. Security is about reassurance that connection and resources are and will remain available. When you feel secure with someone, it feels as if that person is there for you and will continue to be there for you and that they see you in a warm, compassionate way. Feeling emotionally safe and secure with someone is the foundation of trust in a relationship.

Until safety and security are adequately present, relationship collaboration (e.g., joint decisions, projects) won't work as well, and healthy communication will be difficult to manage. This exercise will help you explore and identify what it takes for you to feel safe and secure in the midst of a stressful interaction. You might begin by thinking of a specific interaction you had with a relationship partner when your anxious feelings made communication difficult or unproductive.

What can *you* do to soothe your feelings of threat when communication becomes difficult? (Think mainly of things that help your *body* calm down when it is in a state of distress.)

1. _____

2. _____

3. _____

What kinds of things can your partner do to help you soothe feelings of threat? (Again, focus on your body.)

1. _____

2. _____

3. _____

Because difficult communication can activate feelings of insecurity, what can *you* do to soothe your feelings of insecurity and reassure yourself of the relationship connection?

1. _____

2. _____

3. _____

What kinds of things can *your partner* do or say to help reassure you of the relationship connection?

1. _____

2. _____

3. _____

Now, find time to sit down with your partner or loved one, share what you've learned about safety and security, and explore the lists you came up with. The following prompts may guide you through a useful discussion.

- From what you know about me, how effectively do you think the listed items would soothe me?
- Is there anything you'd add to any of these lists?
- Are you willing to help me with any of these things when you recognize that I'm being reactive?

Effective, healthy communication is possible for anxiously attached people, and developing these skills can help you develop and build trust and safety in your close relationships.

Appreciation Journal

Appreciation is a wonderful way to build up your relationship capital. You and your partner will feel good spending time acknowledging the ways that you make each other's lives better.

List three things you appreciate about your relationship partner:

1. _____

2. _____

3. _____

List three things you appreciate about yourself:

1. _____

2. _____

3. _____

Taking time to appreciate each other on a regular basis can build goodwill and help ease you through difficult moments. By focusing on appreciation, understanding, and acceptance and by learning healthy communication, anxiously attached individuals can build strong, healthy relationships in which both people feel safe and secure.

Avoidance Inventory

Listed below are emotions and circumstances that come up in relationships that many have reported can feel stressful. Look through the list and identify which ones are stressful for you. Circle all the experiences that make you shy away, withdraw, distract, numb out, and in general feel less connected to the people around you. If you think of others that aren't on the list, write them in the blank spaces.

I'm stressed when I feel . . .

Annoyed	Disappointed	Judged
Anxious	Disgusted	Lonely
Ashamed	Dismissed	Longing/desirous
Betrayed	Envious	Pushed to a limit
Blamed	Guilt ridden	Regretful
Burdened	Helpless	Rejected
Condemning	Humiliated	Resentful
Confused	Hurt	Sad
Contemptuous	Ignored	Self-doubting
Criticized	Inadequate	Stressed
Defeated	Indignant	Unappreciated
Demeaned	Intimidated	Uncomfortable
Devastated	Intolerant	Worried
Diminished	Jealous	_____
_____	_____	_____

I'm stressed when I want/need . . .

Support	Affection/warmth	Appreciation
Safety	Stability	Consistency
Acceptance	To be seen and heard	Fairness/mutuality
Calm/harmony	Joyful connection	To be taken seriously
Structure/order	Security	Relief from duties

_____ _____ _____

It's stressful when the relationship requires . . .

Me to self-disclose	Conflict management	Repair from injury
Me to provide emotional support	Clarifying commitment and agreements	Me to understand my partner
Collaborative decision making	Positive ritual and routine	Managing other relationships
Agreement accountability	Boundary defining	Giving evaluation and/or receiving feedback

_____ _____ _____

I get stressed when I fear . . .

Losing autonomy	Losing free time	Losing my identity
Being replaced	Being abandoned	Being excluded

_____ _____ _____

Nice work! You've just identified the kinds of events that activate your avoidant attachment. Now, go through your selections and list the top three things that cause you to withdraw. You will work with these three specific *triggers* in the next exercise.

1. _____

2. _____

3. _____

Avoidance Pros and Cons

Now, you're going to work with the top three *triggers* for withdrawal or avoidance you identified in the last exercise. Write one trigger at the top of each of the following three tables. Then make a check mark by each reaction you have in response. Finally, you'll explore the ways these behaviors help and hurt your relationships.

1. _____

When this happens, I . . .

☐ Withdraw

☐ Ignore

☐ Distract/stay busy

☐ Numb out/leave

☐ Dismiss myself or others

☐ Deny my experience or others'

☐ Justify/rationalize

☐ Explain something irrelevant

☐ Appease without follow-through

☐ Other: _____

What do I gain by doing these things?

_____

_____

What do I miss out on by doing these things?

_____

_____

What is a more constructive response to this trigger?

_____

_____

2. _____

When this happens, I . . .

☐ Withdraw

☐ Ignore

☐ Distract/stay busy

☐ Numb out/leave

☐ Dismiss myself or others

☐ Deny my experience or others'

☐ Justify/rationalize

☐ Explain something irrelevant

☐ Appease without follow-through

☐ Other: _____

What do I gain by doing these things?

_____

_____

What do I miss out on by doing these things?

_____

_____

What is a more constructive response to this trigger?

_____

_____

3. _____

When this happens, I . . .

- ☐ Withdraw
- ☐ Ignore
- ☐ Distract/stay busy
- ☐ Numb out/leave
- ☐ Dismiss myself or others
- ☐ Deny my experience or others'
- ☐ Justify/rationalize
- ☐ Explain something irrelevant
- ☐ Appease without follow-through
- ☐ Other: _____

What do I gain by doing these things?

_____

_____

What do I miss out on by doing these things?

_____

_____

What is a more constructive response to this trigger?

_____

_____

Remember that all of these behaviors were learned. None of them is your fault, but the consequences of these behaviors *are* your business. If you're satisfied with how these reactions are working for you, then carry on! If you're no longer okay with the results, it's in your power to change the behaviors that cause them.

The Effect on You

Think of a time you needed help or support from someone specific, and they either were absent or were there but didn't feel entirely present.

What was the incident?

_____

_____

_____

What do you remember feeling?

_____

_____

_____

What thoughts do you remember having?

_____

_____

_____

How did your body hold that experience?

_____

_____

_____

Empathy in Action

This exercise can be helpful when you're faced with avoidant behavior that leaves you feeling disappointed or let down. Think of a specific time in your life when someone important felt absent or less engaged when you needed them. Pick an incident that isn't too activating in the present moment.

A time someone important to me left me feeling alone was . . .

_____

_____

_____

Instead of what they did, I wanted them to . . .

_____

_____

_____

The situation was stressful for them, because they have a difficult time with . . .

_____

_____

_____

I know this is stressful for them, because . . .

_____

_____

_____

They judged themselves or believed that I judged them as _____. But in reality, they are still learning how to _____, and they are not always perfect at it. When they get overwhelmed, they can _____. They react from reflex instead and forget how much I need them.

You might practice this with a number of incidents; with practice, you'll develop an approach to dealing with these incidents in real time, and you may also develop a greater understanding of and empathy for your avoidant partner.

Exploring Needs and Wants

Now, explore an issue that you don't feel totally fulfilled by in a specific relationship. If nothing comes to mind that strongly, just make a best guess. The point is to explore your thoughts and desires as they relate to that particular relationship.

When I think about this relationship, the thing I don't feel satisfied by is . . .

_____

_____

_____

_____

What would make me happy is . . .

_____

_____

_____

_____

If I got what I wanted, I would feel . . .

_____

_____

_____

_____

How will it affect my relationship in the long term if I never advocate for myself on this issue?

_____

_____

_____

_____

RATING SCALE: *How much effort am I willing to make to assert myself on this issue? (Circle)*

Very little   **Complete**

Secure versus Insecure Approach

In this exercise, you'll have a chance to pick a decision you've made within a relationship and explore the reasons for making the decision based on secure attachment or insecure attachment.

Fill out your own worksheet, beginning with a decision that you've already made pertaining to a relationship. Then put your thoughts and feelings about the decision in the appropriate column, Secure or Insecure. Next, fill out thoughts and feelings that would fit the other category, even if they are hypothetical. The point is to practice identifying whether thoughts and feelings emerge from a secure or an insecure place.

Decision	
My Decision is:	
Insecure approach:	Secure approach:

Questions to consider:

1. What conditions help you have a secure approach to a relationship?
2. What conditions promote an insecure approach?

Imagine a Secure Interaction with Conflict

Most of us get so caught up in the fast pace of conflict that we sometimes don't notice when the other person is offering an olive branch. When these moments are missed, fights last longer and are more stressful.

Recall a time when you were involved with a difficult relationship conflict that didn't go so well, and the other person reacted out of fear or hurt. Remember what this was like—the feelings, thoughts, and body sensations that you experienced in response.

What did the other person do that triggered your reaction?

_____

_____

_____

_____

Now, imagine that the other person can think and feel beyond themselves, instead of just being scared or hurt, and can make an effort to really see your perspective, as well. Imagine the other person as their most generous and compassionate self. The person speaks to you calmly and looks at you with a warm sparkle in their eye. What do you feel now?

_____

_____

_____

_____

You probably felt better. This is what happens when we feel that the person we care about can consider us. If so, really let that good feeling in. Now, imagine showing appreciation for the different response. How would you show your appreciation and encourage the other person to keep doing what you see and hear them doing?

_____

_____

_____

Relationship Strengths

What are your strengths and your partner's? As you interact with someone who has a secure attachment style, it can be helpful to remind yourself of your relationship strengths. Think about what you each contribute to the relationship and gifts that you share with one another. If you're not working on a romantic relationship right now, think in terms of whichever significant relationship you have in mind, whether that's a parent, sibling, best friend, or someone else.

Now that you've picked a specific relationship, go down the column for "Me" and place a check mark by each trait that is a strength you contribute to the relationship. Then go down the column for "My relationship partner" and do the same for the strengths they bring.

The ways in which you each contribute to the relationship may be the same or very different. If they're different, try to acknowledge that some of the ways in which your partner shares those skills and talents may feel unfamiliar at times. If so, try to be open to the new feeling of receiving them in this way, little by little.

Me	My relationship partner	Strengths
		Honesty
		Fairness
		Willingness to put in hard work/effort
		Empathy
		Willingness to be open
		Trustworthiness
		Being a source of inspiration
		Commitment
		Collaboration
		Acceptance of faults
		Providing support
		Perseverance through rough times
		Dependability
		Consistency
		Ability to challenge the other in positive ways
		Playfulness
		Humor
		Readiness to express gratitude and appreciation
		Willingness to sacrifice
		Other:
		Other:

Resources

Books on Attachment and Relationships

- *We Do: Saying Yes to a Relationship of Depth, True Connection, and Enduring Love,* by Stan Tatkin
- *Attached: The New Science of Adult Attachment and How It Can Help You Find—and Keep—Love,* by Amir Levine and Rachel S. F. Heller
- *Conscious Lesbian Dating and Love: A Roadmap to Finding the Right Partner and Creating the Relationship of Your Dreams,* by Ruth L. Schwartz and Michelle Murrain
- *How to Be an Adult in Relationships: The Five Keys to Mindful Loving,* by David Richo
- *The New Rules of Marriage: What You Need to Know to Make Love Work,* by Terrence Real
- *The Power of Attachment: How to Create Deep and Lasting Intimate Relationships,* by Diane Poole Heller

Recommended Workbook

- *The Self-Compassion Skills Workbook: A 14-Day Plan to Transform Your Relationship with Yourself,* by Tim Desmond

Intensive Retreats

- Hoffman Process, www.hoffmaninstitute.org
- Wired for Love & Wired for Relationship Retreats, www.thepactinstitute.com

References

Bowlby, John. *A Secure Base: Parent-Child Attachment and Healthy Human Development.* New York: Basic Books, 1988.

Fosha, Diana, Daniel J. Siegel, and Marion F. Solomon, eds. *The Healing Power of Emotion: Affective Neuroscience, Development, and Clinical Practice.* New York: Norton, 2009.

Gottman, John M. *The Marriage Clinic: A Scientifically Based Marital Therapy.* New York: Norton, 1999.

King, Larry. "Donald and Melania Trump as Newlyweds." Interview, *Larry King Live,* CNN, May 17, 2005. Video, 16:02. https://www.youtube.com/watch?v=q4XfyYFa9yo.

Nummenmaa, Lauri, Enrico Glerean, Riitta Hari, and Jari K. Hietanen. "Bodily Maps of Emotions," *Proceedings of the National Academy of Sciences of the United States of America* 111, no. 2 (January 2014): 646–51. https://doi.org/10.1073/pnas.1321664111.

Porges, Stephen. *"The Neurophysiology of Trauma, Attachment, Self-Regulation and Emotions: Clinical Applications of the Polyvagal Theory."* Online seminar, April 8, 2016. Available from https://www.pesi.com/.

Schore, Judith R., and Allan N. Schore. "Modern Attachment Theory: The Central Role of Affect Regulation in Development and Treatment," *Clinical Social Work Journal* 36, no. 1 (March 2008): 9–20. https://doi:10.1007/s10615-007-0111-7.

Sroufe, Alan, and Daniel Siegel. "The Verdict Is In: The Case for Attachment Theory," *Psychotherapy Networker* 35, no. 2 (March 2011): 35–39.

Tatkin, Stan. *PACT Training Manual: Module One.* Agoura Hills, CA: PACT Institute, 2016.

Index

A

Abandonment, fear of, 20, 31
Acceptance
  of anxious attachment in
    others, 38–39
  of anxious attachment in
    yourself, 34–36
  of avoidant attachment in
    others, 71–73
  of avoidant attachment in
    yourself, 69
  of secure attachment in
    others, 103–104
  of secure attachment in
    yourself, 101–102
Ainsworth, Mary, 5
Anxious attachment
  and acceptance, 34–36, 38–39
  anxious-anxious interaction,
    116–119
  anxious-avoidant interaction,
    126–128
  and empathy, 39–40
  healing from, 142–143
  and healthy communication, 41–45
  how it feels, 21–23
  in others, 28–34
  in relationships, 24–25
  secure-anxious interaction, 129–132
  and self-compassion, 37–38
  traits of, 19–21
  understanding, 26–28
Appreciation, 46
Attachment security, 87. See also
  Secure attachment
Attachment style. See also specific
  discovering personal, 8–15
  interactions, 113–114, 139
  and relationships, 1–2
  stress and, 5–7, 17
Attachment theory, 5–8
Avoidant attachment
  and acceptance, 69–73
  anxious-avoidant interaction,
    126–128
  avoidant-avoidant interaction,
    121–125
  and empathy, 70–73
  healing from, 143–144
  how it feels, 51–54
  in others, 64–68
  in relationships, 55–56
  secure-avoidant interaction, 132–135
  traits of, 49–51, 83
  understanding, 57–63

B

Boundaries, 118–119
Bowlby, John, 5

C

Communication
  conflict, 73–79, 99–101
  consent, 42–43
  eye contact, 138
  healthy, 41
  intimate discussions, 134–135
  "I statements," 106–109
  nonverbal, 118–119, 138
  "quiet love," 138
  safety and security in, 44–46
Connection, feelings of
  appreciation, 46
  perspective, 80–82
  support and nourishment,
    109–110
Consent, 42–43

D

Distance-pursuer dynamic, 126
Domestic violence, 2

E

Emotions, 35–36. See also Feelings
Empathy, 39–40
Expressiveness, 28–29

F

Feelings, 121–125.

G

Gottman, John, 24

I

Insecure anxious attachment, 5, 17.
  See also Anxious attachment
Insecure avoidant attachment, 5, 17.
  See also Avoidant attachment

N

National Domestic Violence
  Hotline, 2
Needs, 44–46, 76–77, 88–89

P

Playfulness, 115, 128
Porges, Stephen, 128
Pseudosecurity, 93–95

R

Relationship capital, 24, 25
Relationships. See also
  Communication
  anxious attachment and, 24–25,
    28–34
  avoidant attachment and, 55–56,
    64–68
  building healthy, 141–142
  consent in, 42–43
  positive values in, 4
  recognizing burnout in, 30–31
  safety and security in, 44–46
  secure attachment in, 92–96
  security in, 1–2, 17, 90–91, 139
  strengths in, 104–106
  violence in, 2
Rituals, 131–132

S

Safety needs, 44–45
Secure attachment
  and acceptance, 101–104
  how it feels, 87–89
  vs. insecure attachment, 97–98
  lasting, 144–146
  in others, 93–96
  promoting, 90–91
  in relationships, 92
  research on, 5–6
  responding to, 99–101
  secure-anxious interaction, 129–132
  secure-avoidant interaction, 132–135
  secure-secure interaction, 135–138
  traits of, 85–87
Security needs, 44–46
Self-compassion, 37–38
Self-criticism, 102
Stress, and attachment style, 5–7, 17

T

Tatkin, Stan, 93
Triggers
  anxious attachment, 26–28
  avoidant attachment, 57–63
Trump, Donald, 119
Trump, Melania, 119

V

Values, 131–132

W

Window of tolerance, 66–67
Withdrawal, negative responses to, 68

Acknowledgments

I am eternally grateful to my mentor and teacher, Stan Tatkin, who has taught me how safety and security are indispensable to being a human in relationships. I continue to be inspired by his brilliant and powerful work, which pushes me to be a better therapist, writer, and relationship partner.

Thank you to the ancestors for their blessings. I owe everything to my mother, Yue Chang Chen, and brother, Addison Chen, who support me, evolve with me, and show me how family sticks together.

Thank you to everyone who gave their time to develop the attachment self-assessment. Their fresh input was exactly what I needed when I was engrossed with deadlines. The quiz, and book, would not be what it is without them all. Many thanks to Diana Wu, Julio Rios, Tamara Chellam, Alexander Aris, Evan Schloss, Vanessa Diaz, and Mona Kim.

Finally, I credit my editors for helping me share this work with more people. Camille Hayes gave me the opportunity to write my first book and pulled for the best of what I had to offer. Lori Handelman's editorial touch made the ideas clearer and more balanced. The encouraging words of both made me believe in this book all the more.

About the Author

Annie Chen, LMFT, is a licensed marriage and family therapist with a private practice in Oakland, California, focused on working with couples. She holds master's degrees in counseling and Process Work. Things that make her happy are mushrooms, flax linen, tending her garden, meditation, and small acts of disruption to oppressive systems. If you would like to receive updates from Annie or work with her, visit ChangeInsight.net.